NEGOTIATION BOOT CAMP

ED BRODOW

NEGOTIATION BOOT CAMP

How to Resolve Conflict, Satisfy
Customers, and Make Better Deals

CURRENCY   DOUBLEDAY
New York   London   Toronto   Sydney   Auckland

A CURRENCY BOOK
PUBLISHED BY DOUBLEDAY

Published in the United States by Doubleday, an imprint of The
Doubleday Broadway Publishing Group, a division of Random
House, Inc., New York.
www.currencybooks.com

CURRENCY is a trademark of Random House, Inc., and DOUBLEDAY is a
registered trademark of Random House, Inc.

Negotiation Boot Camp™ is a registered trademark.
All trademarks are the property of their respective companies.

Book design by Michael Collica

Library of Congress Cataloging-in-Publication Data

Brodow, Ed.
Negotiation boot camp : how to resolve conflict, satisfy customers,
and make better deals / Ed Brodow.—1st ed.
        p. cm.
"A Currency book."
Includes bibliographical references and index.
1. Negotiation in business. I. Title.

HD58.6B75 2006
658.4'052—dc22

2006019748

ISBN: 978-0-385-51849-9

PRINTED IN THE UNITED STATES OF AMERICA

SPECIAL SALES
Currency Books are available at special discounts for bulk purchases
for sales promotions or premiums. Special editions, including
personalized covers, excerpts of existing books, and corporate
imprints, can be created in large quantities for special needs. For more
information, write to Special Markets, Currency Books,
specialmarkets@randomhouse.com

10 9 8 7 6 5 4 3 2 1

First Edition

Contents

Contents

At Doubleday, thanks to Roger Scholl for imagining this book and for being creative, supportive, and just a downright pleasure to work with; to Talia Krohn for her insightful editing that made me go "WOW"; and to John Fontana for his smashing cover design.

Thanks to Ellen Levine at Trident Media Group for doing her magic once again.

Thanks to the *Boys from Brooklyn*: Barry Wishner, Dr. Sam Hessel, Chairman Harvey Pitt, the Hon. Joel Blumenfeld, and Richard Brook, Esq.

Thanks to the ongoing support, moral and otherwise, from Jeffrey Gitomer, Dr. Fred Berke, Dr. Robert Luthardt, Barbara Wishner, Joseph P. Wilson, Caroline Hunt, Eric Foumberg, Christopher Cayce, Linda Purdy, Ed Collins, Mark Oman, Dr. David Starr, Jennifer de St. Georges, Marjorie Brody, Ivy Naistadt, Theo Androus, Elizabeth Mello, Jeff Salz, Emory Austin, and my literary mentor, Susan Page.

Thanks to all my loyal clients for making Negotiation Boot Camp™ the seminar of choice.

Thanks to my giant-bird-of-paradise plant, Bubba, for not complaining that I spent too much time writing this book.

NEGOTIATION BOOT CAMP

BOOT CAMP INDUCTION

Everything I Know about Negotiation
I Learned in Brooklyn

A decent boldness ever meets with friends.
—HOMER, *ODYSSEY*

People who have mastered the art of negotiation often have an easier time on this planet than the millions of lost souls who have not. That is why, in 1994, I created the Negotiation Boot Camp™ seminar. Informed by my experience as sales executive and corporate negotiator in the computer and telecommunications industries and as CEO of my own company, the seminar was designed to provide customized negotiation training for corporate clients. These clients have included Microsoft, The Hartford, Starbucks, Goldman Sachs, Seagate, Philip Morris, Raytheon, The Gap, Cisco Systems, and Kimberly-Clark.

"I learned more in one day of Negotiation Boot Camp than I did in my entire two-year Stanford MBA program," confessed a newly enlightened manager at a major Silicon Valley computer company. Negotiation Boot Camp provided her with everything she needed to make her way in the world. Now, by reading this book, you too can benefit from the insights that have helped countless others improve their careers and their lives through successful negotiation.

Yet, how significant a difference a good negotiator can make is often brought into question. Some people believe that every deal has a "perfect outcome" that will be reached no matter what the negotiators do. This has not been my experience. Every negotiation has a unique outcome not only because the circumstances differ, but also because the negotiators bring different skill sets to the table. Without exception, the practice negotiations in my seminars have yielded a wide range of outcomes. The single variable that accounts for the difference is the negotiating ability of the individual participants.

How, you may ask, does this apply to the real world? One of my clients, a software company, was curious about whether the money it spent on negotiation training was worth it. By tracking the average selling price of its products before and after I trained its sales force, this is what my client found out: Before I showed up, the salespeople were caving in to customer demands right and left. Profits were hurting. In the year after I taught them the correct way to negotiate a sale, *the company's average selling price went up by an extraordinary 59 percent!*

The way you negotiate really does matter. Among the factors that may influence the outcome of your negotiations: how well you read the other side's situation and manage its expectations; where you open and what concessions you make; how you respond to the other side's tactics; and the point at which you decide to either make a deal or walk away. Never underestimate the importance of your negotiating ability.

You may be wondering where I acquired my negotiation savvy. The answer, in a single word, is Brooklyn.

Brooklyn, in case you didn't know, is the largest borough of New York City, with a population of about 3 million. It has always been, and still is, a melting pot of races, nationalities, and religions. It has been estimated that one in four Americans can trace their ancestry back to Brooklyn. I have what I call an MBA: Master of Brooklyn Acumen.

Brooklyn has always been a tough school. Growing up in my neighborhood, negotiation skills were essential survival equipment. Here is an example. Imagine you are walking down a poorly lit Brooklyn street late at night and three thugs jump you. They are bigger than you are, and possibly armed. Do you fight your way out of it? Not a good idea. No, if you want to get away unharmed, and even possibly keep *some* of the contents of your wallet, you talk your way out of it. This is one way that negotiators are born.

Let me tell you a story. When I was sixteen, I flew across the country to visit relatives in California. During this visit, my aunt and uncle took me and my seven-year-old cousin Howard on a drive to Tijuana, Mexico. Decades later, Howard still recalls a negotiation I had with a Mexican shop owner over a toy donkey.

"You kept refusing to pay his price," says Howard. "You got him to bring the price down lower and lower and lower. Eventually the man became so flustered that he offered to give you the toy for nothing. I was amazed that you were able to handle this veteran shopkeeper with such dexterity."

"What's the big deal?" I inquire every time he tells the story.

"You were only sixteen!" Howard retorts. "How the hell were you able to do that? I'm in my forties and I still can't!"

Not so. Howard only *thinks* he can't do it. He thinks this because, as an average American, he has been poisoned by several false assumptions:

1. The average person is not tough enough to win at negotiation.
2. Negotiation is all-or-nothing. You are either a winner or a loser.
3. Only good talkers make good negotiators.
4. Assertive people are selfish and rude.
5. Women do not negotiate as effectively as men.

Let's examine these destructive assumptions.

ASSUMPTION NUMBER 1: *The average person is not tough enough to win at negotiation.*

You don't have to be Donald Trump—or any other larger-than-life personality whose aggressive boardroom style reduces his adversaries to simpering, blubbering idiots—to win at negotiation. What people don't realize is that subtlety can be equally effective in a negotiation. By reading this book you'll learn that you don't have to be the class bully to get what you want—you just need to understand the rules of negotiation and how to manipulate them. Anyone can be a successful negotiator if they do their homework and pay attention to a few basic rules.

ASSUMPTION NUMBER 2: *Negotiation is all-or-nothing. You are either a winner or a loser.*

Contrary to popular belief, negotiation is not really about winning, it is about collaborating.

The majority of my Negotiation Boot Camp™ seminar attendees admit that, in the past, they have not enjoyed negotiating. I have always maintained that this negative attitude simply stems from the perception that a negotiation is a contest, which can't be won unless someone else loses.

But the thought that someone has to lose can produce anxiety because it means that the person to lose may be you. Some people become consumed by the fear of losing, thinking about what might happen if things don't go their way. Before they know it their stomach is tied up in knots and they feel as if they are going to be sick. This is why so many people hate to negotiate.

Some people believe that Donald Trump is the consummate negotiator. (No doubt The Donald is one of them.) In my Boot Camp seminars, I often use Peter Falk's classic TV detective Columbo as a better role model for a negotiator. Why? Columbo is known for keeping a leash on his own ego. He asks questions, listens to others, and solves problems. Columbo is a reasonable man with a strong sense of humility. His objective is uncovering the truth, not winning a war of egos.

In place of the win-lose model, I propose a collaborative approach to negotiation in which both sides can consider themselves winners. This eliminates the anxiety over the outcome and allows us to enjoy the process.

ASSUMPTION NUMBER 3: *Only good talkers make good negotiators.*

For the first twenty-three years of my life I subscribed to the theory that all successful people are good talkers. Boy, did I have it wrong! The rest of my life has been devoted to the realization that *listening* is really what success is all about. It is the single most important lesson I have learned in decades of doing business. Listening to others is critical for anyone who wants to master the art of negotiation. That's why an entire section of this book is devoted to developing your listening skills.

ASSUMPTION NUMBER 4: *Assertive people are selfish and rude.*

I'm not sure where this fallacy originated. It is absurd to suggest that a person should not look out for himself. Yet society has somehow embraced the notion that assertive people are rude, selfish, and socially undesirable. Not long ago I was sitting in a Los Angeles restaurant with several acquaintances. We were upset because the waitress was neglecting our table, but when I called out to the waitress they chastised me. *Don't make a scene!* They preferred the bad service to my assertive behavior. In their eyes I was out of line. In my eyes, their passivity was ridiculous.

Never apologize for trying to get your needs met. If you don't take care of yourself, you are in no position to help anyone else. Consider the instructions they give in case of emergency on an airplane: "In case of a loss of cabin pressure, put on your own oxygen mask before assisting the person next to you." Taking care of Number One first just makes sense.

Being assertive ensures that your needs are met. And this is what negotiation is all about.

ASSUMPTION NUMBER 5: *Women do not negotiate as effectively as men.*

It is often suggested that men are more aggressive than women. Women are thought to be more passive and therefore ill equipped for confrontation. So, some claim, men make better negotiators than women. After conducting seminars on negotiation for twenty years, I have concluded that this is a lot of hooey! Some men are better negotiators than most women. Some women are better than most men. Period.

In this case, generalization only leads to folly. The idea that the sexes are intrinsically different is a sneaky way of placing limitations on women. The important thing, whatever your gender, is to create a negotiation style that is in sync with your own personality. *Negotiation Boot Camp* will help you do that.

Each chapter corresponds to a week of boot camp, totaling twelve weeks. Just like Marine Corps boot camp would train you in the art of being a Marine, *Negotiation Boot Camp* will train you in the art of negotiation. We will begin with the ten traits that all great negotiators have in common. From there you will learn how to prepare for negotiation and how to create your own strategy. Negotiation usually involves give-and-take, so you will be schooled in the rules of concession-making. You will then review a series of negotiation tactics (but keep in mind that negotiation is more about attitude than it is about "tricks").

All negotiations involve buying and selling in one form or another. In some negotiations you will be both buyer *and* seller. So we will examine the negotiation process from the standpoint of buyers as well as sellers. We will also consider the importance of negotiation on employee/manager relationships. In today's world you will often have occasion to negotiate with people from other cultures. I will share tips for negotiating with people whose cultural orientations may differ from yours.

Finally, I will work to expand your negotiation consciousness by arming you with the skills to negotiate for things that you never knew were negotiable—your salary, department store purchases, and medical bills.

By the end of the book you will be ready to approach any negotiation—in business or in your personal life—with confidence and skill.

Ed Brodow
Monterey, California
www.NegotiationBootCamp.com

Is There a Negotiator in Your Closet?

The fault, dear Brutus, is not in our stars, but in ourselves.
—SHAKESPEARE, *JULIUS CAESAR*

Conflict seems to be part of the human condition. Regardless of what the issue is, we will find a way to fight over it. In spite of this tendency, human beings have always tried to get along. What is the greatest invention in history: Fire? The wheel? $E = mc^2$? In my view, it is the art of negotiation. Negotiation is about getting along.

Let me give you my definition of negotiation:

Negotiation is the process of overcoming obstacles in order to reach agreement.

What is the primary obstacle? The difference between your position and my position. Human beings invented negotiation to stop ourselves from physically harming each other (or worse) when our respective positions appear to be incompatible. The history of conflict resolution from the last ice age to the present suggests that without the art of negotiation, the human population would be significantly smaller.

The objective of negotiating is to reach agreement. So in one sense, a successful negotiation is one that culminates in agreement. There are times, however, as we will see, when the *lack* of agreement—an *impasse* or *deadlock*—can signal a successful outcome; that is, *if* we determine that, in this particular instance, an agreement is not in our best interest.

All things considered, I prefer to think of a successful negotiation as one in which at least one of the parties is satisfied with the outcome. *Satisfaction* is the key element in every successful negotiation. In a traditional adversarial negotiation, such as the sale of a house, the negotiation is successful if *you* are satisfied. In a cooperative (win-win) negotiation, success occurs when *both parties* are satisfied.

One point of clarification here. *Satisfaction* means that you get what you *need,* not necessarily what you *want.* What you *need* and what you *want* are not always the same thing. You need a car to get to work. You want a Lexus or a Mercedes, but your budget won't stretch that far. A Honda will do the job. So your need is met and you can be satisfied with a Honda.

There is also an important difference between your *need* and your stated *position.* Your need is what you must get in order to solve a problem. Your position, on the other hand, is what you *say you want.* Occasionally, a negotiator may put forth a position that asks for more than she truly needs. Satisfaction occurs when the need is met, not when a position is satisfied. In a negotiation, instead of being sidetracked by positions, it is essential to focus on the other negotiator's needs.

PROFILE OF A NEGOTIATOR

I believe the kind of negotiation we should strive for is one in which both parties achieve satisfaction. What kind of negotiator is able to make this happen? Can we create a profile for the successful negotiator?

Below are the ten traits I've found that successful negotiators tend to have. *How many of them do you share?*

1. Negotiation Consciousness

We've all heard the phrase "Everything is negotiable." In the world of negotiation, my world, that is literally true. *Negotiation consciousness* is what I call the mind-set of people who make deals. A person who has high negotiation consciousness tends to be assertive in stating what he wants and challenges everything. And that means *everything.* You cannot achieve what you want in a negotiation if you are unwilling to challenge the other person's position.

The classic example of low negotiation consciousness is often seen in the area of contract negotiations. Even the most experienced buyers and sellers are intimidated by contract clauses. The majority of contracts are written by attorneys in complex legal language that most people are afraid to challenge. A negotiator with high negotiation consciousness is not scared to challenge contract clauses, even if she does not completely understand the legal jargon.

In one eye-opening instance, I was hired as a speaker for a large corporation. The contract they wanted me to sign included a clause that required me to take out millions of dollars in liability insurance. I immediately pointed out to my client that I was merely the guest speaker, and since the facilities were under the sole control of the client, there was no earthly reason for me to be held liable for any injuries that might occur as I gave my speech.

"I'm sorry," replied my client. "It is company policy. I don't have the authority to change it."

I guess they expected me to concede and let the issue die. Instead, I asked to speak to the head of the contracts department, who gave me the same speech. "It's our policy, blah, blah, blah." Still, I would not back down. I pursued the issue all the way to the legal department at the company's headquarters in another state. When I explained the problem to their head lawyer, she agreed with me.

"This obviously does not apply to you," she said. "Go ahead and strike the clause from the contract."

Without negotiation consciousness, I would have been at the mercy of a piece of paper.

A client of mine recently admitted to having low negotiation consciousness.

"I just don't like to be assertive," she said.

It seems she had called her accountant and asked a short, simple question. Although the call lasted only ten minutes, she soon received a bill for $250. When she called about the bill, her accountant said, "My policy is to charge $250 for all phone calls."

"But you've been my accountant for ten years," said my client, "and in all that time, you've never charged me for phone calls."

"It's a new policy," he replied.

My client was too intimidated to argue. "How can I overcome my passivity?" she asked me.

"Being aware of your low negotiation consciousness is the first step," I replied. "Now you must compensate for your weakness in this area by making a special effort to be assertive."

Undoubtedly, people had been taking advantage of this accountant by engaging him in long phone conversations and expecting that they would not be charged. So I advised my client: "Tell him that you can understand why he was upset, but that (a) you didn't know his policy had changed, (b) your call was only ten minutes, and (c) you will be happy to comply with his policy with respect to future calls."

"Do you think I can really change my character?" my client wondered.

"It is not about changing your character," I explained. "It is about *changing your behavior*. You simply need to be more willing to challenge what other people tell you."

Challenging means not taking things at face value. Instead of blindly accepting other people's assumptions, you have to be able to think for yourself.

This applies when you are buying a new car. Don't just accept the sticker price; instead, use it as the starting point for your negotiation.

And it applies when your accountant bills you $250 for a ten-minute phone call.

When a negotiator is confronted with a contrary point of view, his attitude is, "That's your opinion. Here's mine." Having the guts to speak up is called *assertiveness*. Being assertive means asking for what you want and refusing to take "no" for an answer. Here are my Assertiveness Training Tips that may help you change your behavior:

a. **Ask.** If you don't ask, you won't get your needs met. Pay attention to the way that children ask for things. They are more aware than adults of the connection between needs and survival. Adults will often feel guilty about asking for the things they need. There are three conditions under which I believe it is critical that you stand up for what you want:

- When the stakes are high. If it is a matter of great importance, be persistent. ╱
- When the amount of money involved is more than you want to lose. ╱
- When what you are asking for is simply fair and the other person's position is unreasonable, or does not make sense.

b. **Eliminate negative self-talk.** Our minds are full of self-doubt that limits our ability to be assertive, by telling us what we can't do, what we're not supposed to want. The antidote to such self-doubt is self-awareness. Each time you are aware of a negative thought, replace it with a positive one. If you hear yourself saying, "They'll never say yes," try substituting, "If I ask for what I want, I have a good chance of getting it." The more aware you are of your negative thoughts, the easier it will be to replace them with positive ones.

c. **Practice expressing your feelings without anxiety or anger.** When you fail to express your legitimate feelings, you are relinquishing your power to the other person. Let people know what you want in a nonthreatening way by practicing "I" statements. For example, instead of saying, "You shouldn't do that," try substituting, "I don't feel comfortable when you do that." When you use an "I" statement, you are taking responsibility for your feelings as opposed to attacking the other person.

d. **Learn to say NO.** People overstep our boundaries all the time. They try to bully us into giving them what they want. But others can't bully or intimidate you if you are comfortable saying NO. Set limits and boundaries, and don't allow other people to cross them. If you are the kind of person who typically says YES as a first response, you can fight that urge by giving yourself time before you respond. Try saying, "Let me get back to you on that" instead of saying yes automatically.

Remember, there is a difference between being assertive and being aggressive. You are being assertive when you take care of your own interests while maintaining respect for the interests of others. When you pursue your own interests without regard for other people, you are aggressive. I am promoting assertiveness, not aggression, in your relationships with others.

2. Listening

Sadly, our culture is full of people who don't know how to listen. Last week I experienced some difficulty in getting my car to start, so I took it to the automobile dealer. "When I turn the key in the ignition, it starts to turn over and then stops," I told the service manager. They "fixed" it. A few days later the problem reoccurred. I took the car to the dealer again. It seems that the service manager had written on the service ticket, "Funny noise when starting." He had not paid attention to what I said. I never mentioned a funny noise. As a result, the service technician had not done the job correctly, and the car had to be serviced again to address the actual problem. Had the manager listened correctly the first time, a return visit would have been unnecessary. This kind of situation happens all the time. Most people are terrible listeners. Imagine how much this kind of sloppy behavior costs businesses everywhere.

After negotiation consciousness, the most important trait of successful negotiators is the ability to listen. Among the benefits of listening are:

- You will learn the other negotiator's needs and pressures.
- You will discover where your own strength lies.
- The person you are negotiating with will like you and want to help you. Human beings respond positively to other human beings who listen.
- You will discover how to get your needs met.

Week Two of *Negotiation Boot Camp* is devoted to the ABCs of listening.

3. The Ability to Ask Good Questions

Good negotiators are like detectives. What do detectives do? They ask questions. The service manager at my car dealership should have asked, "Does your car make a noise when you start the engine?" Asking questions goes hand in hand with listening. By asking the right questions and then listening to the answers, you can find out what is driving the other side of the negotiation.

4. High Aspirations

After conducting Negotiation Boot Camp seminars for hundreds of corporate clients and sales organizations, I am convinced of this fact: Salespeople who are able to sell consistently at higher prices genuinely believe in the value of what they are selling. They know their product is superior and they *expect a higher reward* for it. A seller with high negotiation consciousness and high aspirations will ignore a buyer's attempts to lowball. In one instance, as I described earlier, we were able to nearly double the average sales price at a computer software company by teaching the sales force to maintain high aspirations by selling the value—not the price—of their software product.

The lesson is clear: Negotiators who have high aspirations do better. Successful negotiators are optimists. They expect to succeed. In a negotiation, your level of expectation becomes a self-fulfilling prophecy.

This rule applies not only to sellers, but to buyers as well. In my Negotiation Boot Camp seminars, I run a series of role-playing exercises. In one, the group is divided into buyers and sellers. The buyers are asked, "What is the most you are willing to pay, under pressure, for the seller's product or service?" The sellers are asked, "What is the least you will accept, under pressure, from the buyer for your product or service?" A clear correlation exists between the expectations of the negotiators and what they are able to achieve in the negotiation that follows. Buyers who aim high—their intention is to pay less—generally pay less than the average buyer in the group. Sellers who aim high—their intention is to sell at higher prices—generally sell at higher prices than the average seller.

5. Patience

Impatience is the American disease. As we are inundated with more and more information, we get more and more impatient. The MTV generation just wants to get its information as quickly as possible. In negotiation, this can be fatal. There are two reasons why you should take your time:

1. Whoever is more patient is in the driver's seat. Being patient will force the other side to give in as their anxiety rises.
2. If you slow down, you'll make fewer mistakes.

The next time you buy a new car, try spending some time in the showroom talking with the salesperson. Then go home and process the information you received. Come back a few days later and repeat the process. If the salesperson has not made quota, or if the dealership needs the sale, you will probably receive a more generous offer.

Anyone who has negotiated in Asia, the Middle East, or South America will tell you that people in these cultures look at time differently than we do in North America and Europe. During an extended trip to South America, at first I was frustrated at how long it took to get anything done. It angered me, for example, that dinner in my hotel took two hours. Eventually, though, I came to relish these long dinners and realize that their way of eating is a healthier way. The dinners prepared me for the South American style of negotiation, which, in stark contrast to the brisk American approach, allows plenty of time for the parties to get to know and trust each other. And I began to appreciate that the more time we take in negotiation, the fewer mistakes we are likely to make.

There is an old saying, "Marry in haste, repent in leisure." The same is true of negotiation. "Negotiate in haste, repent in leisure."

6. Flexibility

When we negotiate, we make all kinds of assumptions about the other side's needs, wants, goals, options, pressures, strategies, and so on. The problem with assumptions is that they can be wrong. If you make assumptions and then refuse to change them as new information comes to light, you will be trapped in your own rigid position.

Here are some typical assumptions made by business negotiators:

- "I don't have a chance; they hold all the cards."
- "The buyer will never accept my price increase."
- "The seller will never accept my low offer."
- "If I walk away from the table, the other side will give up."
- "The other side has no viable alternatives."

When we make these assumptions, we don't know if they are correct. We merely *think* they are correct. Successful negotiators always make assumptions, but they are flexible enough to change them in response to changing circumstances.

The Asian concept of "saving face" is one way, though not always the best way, of dealing with changing circumstances. With a face-saving excuse, the negotiator can change course without admitting that he has made a mistake. I witnessed a Japanese businessman use laughter to avoid admitting that he had not understood one section in my proposal for a telecommunications system to be installed in his firm's New York office. I knew I was expected to go along with the deception, so instead of explaining what I could see he hadn't understood, I followed his cue and pretended that a significant part of the proposal did not exist. His face-saving device, the laughter, prevented him from getting the information he needed to correct his wrong assumption. I have always believed we are better off confronting our assumptions, whether they are right or wrong.

7. Focus on Satisfaction

Successful negotiators look at situations from the other side's perspective. My philosophy of negotiation includes the firm belief that one hand washes the other. If I know that you are trying to help me to get my needs met, I will help you. Over the years I have observed that successful negotiators want the other side to get what they want as well. Instead of asking, "How can I win?" they ask, "How can I help the other negotiator feel satisfied?"

During a high-profile insider trading case, the Securities and Exchange Commission made a deal in which the defendant would pay a fine of $100 million to the government in cash and securities. As the deal was being finalized, the SEC was told that the defendant wanted to change the composition of the $100 million package. A portion of the initial package included securities in his own company, valued at $20 million. At the last minute, he decided he did not want to give this up. How would his lawyers negotiate this change of position without blowing the entire settlement?

"We can't include the company," the defendant's lawyers told the SEC.

Several SEC staff members grew angry and red-faced. "You are reneging on your agreement," they asserted.

But, as the attorneys pointed out in response, if the company went under, those securities might turn out to be worthless.

"We don't want to embarrass the Commission by giving you assets that aren't worth what we said they were worth. We would prefer to substitute something that has more substantial value."

The SEC staff was satisfied that the defendant's position was in the SEC's best interest. By framing its position *from the perspective of the SEC*, the defense team was able to win the point while giving the SEC staff a sense of satisfaction.

Everyone looks at the world differently, so when you are negotiating with another person, you are way ahead of the game if you can focus on how that person perceives the situation. I'll talk about this more in Week Six.

8. Willingness to Take Risks

As we have discussed, negotiation consciousness describes a willingness to be assertive and challenge everything. In challenging another person's position, a successful negotiator will take reasonable risks based upon reliable information. Negotiators understand that we all need to take risks. Face it, you wouldn't be alive and reading this if your parents hadn't taken a risk.

Risks lurk in every step of the negotiation process. These risks include asking for more than you think you can get, or giving the other side an ultimatum. Or it can manifest itself in the form of theatricality. Have you ever taken the risk of getting emotional in a negotiation? Next time you buy a car, for example, try some old-fashioned theatrics and threaten to walk out. Think about how you feel when someone else gets emotional, like when you try to fire an employee and he starts to cry. (It happened to me.) It makes you doubt yourself; you think your position must be unreasonable to trigger such an outpouring of emotion. Histrionics can be effective.

When it comes to taking risks, the important question is, "How much risk is justifiable?" My grandfather invested everything he had in the stock market. It must have appeared to him as a reasonable risk at the time. Unfortunately, the year was 1929 and he was wiped out. My grandmother didn't think it was reasonable. She never spoke to him again.

When you take a risk, consider your options if the risk turns sour. Select an upcoming negotiation and ask yourself:

1. "How much risk am I comfortable taking in this negotiation?" If you are selling your house, for example, how long are you willing to hold on before you drop your price? If it's a seller's market, it may be a viable risk to wait until you get your price. If you're in a buyer's market, however, you may want to grab the first warm buyer who comes along with a reasonable offer.

2. "If I take the risk and it doesn't work out the way I hope, what options/alternatives do I have? Do I have a Plan B?" If you lose a buyer for your house because you won't budge on the price, are other buyers likely to come knocking at your door?

Make sure that your risks are reasonable, and that you have a plan of action no matter the outcome.

9. Solving the Problem

All too often negotiations go awry because one or both of the negotiators get sidetracked by personal issues unrelated to the negotiation at hand. After a recent speech to a group of venture capitalists, a member of the audience confessed to me that he had just botched a multimillion-dollar deal because he had become upset by the other negotiator's rude and inconsiderate manner. He had been rude and inconsiderate in response, and the two were unable to reach an agreement.

Successful negotiators don't take things personally. They focus on solving the problems central to the negotiation. If two negotiators don't like each other, they still must find a way to rise above personal feelings in order to make a deal.

In my corporate career I've seen many negotiations that included emotional outbursts. But once all the screaming and yelling stopped, both sides would go out for a pleasant dinner. They were able to leave the emotional posturing at the table because they knew it was just business. If they had taken it personally, they never would have been able to reach agreement.

In one acquisition deal, a tiny one-story building with no

productive value threatened to derail an entire $200 million transaction. The founder of the company up for sale had started the business in this three-room house thirty years earlier—it was known in company circles as the "founding edifice." Both the CEO of the conglomerate that was purchasing the firm and the company's founder were "winner-take-all" tough guys, and so neither wanted to concede ownership of this virtually worthless property. The buyer insisted that it was part of the firm's real estate plant. The seller claimed sentimental value. Neither party would budge. The seller's attorney, in a last-ditch effort to salvage an agreement, said to his client, "Joe, why don't you just take a picture of it?" The seller suddenly recognized the absurdity of his position, put his personal feelings aside, and relented. A $200 million deal had almost gone down the drain over this minuscule issue.

10. Willingness to Walk Away

I call this *Brodow's Law*: Always be willing to walk away. If you want the deal too badly, you lose your ability to say no. Don't place yourself in a position where you accept a less than satisfactory outcome, just to close a deal.

This lesson was lasered onto my consciousness during my sales career, when one of my prospective clients reneged on a promise to sign our contract. Without saying a word, I packed up my briefcase and walked out of his office.

"Where are you going?" he called after me.

"I'm leaving," I said. "You lied to me and I don't want to do business with you."

He chased me all the way to the elevator bank and

begged me to return. He knew he had pushed me as far as I would go, and he agreed to sign the contract.

Afterward he asked me, "Ed, if I hadn't followed you, would you have come back?"

"I guess you'll never know," I told him.

When making a major purchase, such as a car or a house, it often pays *not* to negotiate. A friend once called to confess that she had just purchased a car for more than the sticker price.

Why?

"I just wanted it so badly," she said. She thought it was the perfect car, and it never occurred to her that she might have saved several thousand dollars and been equally satisfied by purchasing a different model, a different color, or a different make of car. Some people see the house they've always wanted and go gaga. "This is my dream house. I will pay anything to get it." To avoid this kind of mistake, you must be willing to say, "If I can't buy this house at a price that I can live with, I will find another dream house."

Let me make this clear: I am not saying that you should always walk away from a negotiation. But if you don't even consider the option of walking away from the negotiation, you may be inclined to cave in to the other side's demands simply to make a deal. If you are not desperate—if you recognize that you have other options—the other negotiator will sense your inner strength. Your *willingness* to walk away is one of the greatest bargaining chips you have.

NEGOTIATION STYLES

Before concluding Week One, I want to discuss what are known as "negotiation styles." While I dislike placing people in categories, there are generally thought to be several "styles" that describe typical negotiation behaviors. You may find that you fall squarely in one of these camps, or that your style is a blend of those described below.

Tough Guys

Tough Guys are ego-driven and need to win. They will try to demonstrate what great negotiators they are by bullying, or using threats, ridicule, and guilt. (Donald Trump falls into this category.) Do you remember how to deal with the schoolyard bully? You have to stand up to him. Punch him in the nose, perhaps. But you don't want to knock him out, because when he comes to, he will be a bigger pain in the neck than before. The same goes for the Tough Guy negotiator. Here is how to handle him:

- Lower his expectations by standing up to him.
- Stroke his ego so he will want to be nice to you.

So, while you're showing him that you won't be intimidated, you should also massage his ego. The TV character Columbo is a classic example of someone who is able to subordinate his own ego to draw out his murder suspect. It works.

Nice Guys

Nice Guys can be deceiving. They may *act* nice, but they can be trickier to deal with than the Tough Guys because when they do get tough, they catch you off guard. When you negotiate with a Tough Guy, at least you know what you are up against. But with a Nice Guy, everything is coming

up roses until you drop your guard and then . . . *kaboom!*
They can hit you below the belt. So don't be taken in by all
the sweetness and smiles. Focus on the issues and keep
your guard up. (An example of a Nice Guy: Martha Stewart.)

Nitpickers

The Nitpicker is detail-oriented. She wants to dot every "i"
and cross every "t." Many buyers are Nitpickers because
they know it drives salespeople crazy. Nitpickers try your
patience by insisting that you go over every last detail, and
by giving you a long list of straw demands (see my discussion in Week Eight). The way to deal with Nitpickers is to
be patient, refuse to allow them to wear you down, and try
to impose a deadline so they don't drag things out forever.

Absentminded Professors

Columbo reminds me of an Absentminded Professor. By acting dumb and goofy, he encourages his murder suspects to
be careless and give themselves away. The Absentminded
Professor may act like he doesn't know what he is doing,
but don't be fooled. If you make the mistake of underesti-
mating him, he will roll over you like a two-ton truck.

Weaklings

These people try to win your sympathy by acting weak.
"I'm in trouble—please help me!" Don't let down your
guard. If you decide to help a Weakling by making concessions, be sure to get at least as many concessions in return.
Like the Absentminded Professor, she may be acting. I think

of Scarlett O'Hara as a classic example. She acts like a Weakling, but underneath, of course, she's one of the toughest and most utterly self-centered characters in cinema history.

The important thing about negotiation style is that you must *develop your own*! But as you do so, remember to focus on the ten essential traits of successful negotiators. The upcoming chapters will teach you how.

Be Nice to Your Ears

I wish people who have trouble communicating would just shut up.
—TOM LEHRER

On the evening of October 30, 1938, hysteria descended upon the United States. Thousands fled their homes in panic. People reported fires, destruction of property, and evidence of death rays. Police phone lines were tied up by the enormous volume of frantic callers, adding fuel to the fire. The American public was convinced that Planet Earth was under attack by Martians!

That evening, at exactly 8:00 P.M. Eastern Standard Time, CBS Radio broadcast the Orson Welles version of H. G. Wells' novel *The War of the Worlds*. At the beginning of the broadcast an announcement was made saying that the program was "a dramatization by the Mercury Theatre."

The announcement was repeated several times during and after the performance. Yet for some peculiar reason, the announcement was missed by hordes of radio fans who heard the broadcast. As a result, they panicked, believing that their lives were indeed at the mercy of space aliens. In Grover's Mill, New Jersey, where the fictional Martian attack was supposedly taking place, many residents packed their cars with valuables and headed out of town. One terrified man fired his shotgun at a windmill, mistaking it for a Martian.

The big question on everyone's mind the next day, once the public learned they were not actually under Martian attack, was: How could this mass hysteria have occurred when CBS had clearly presented the information that it was a theatrical adaptation? The answer: People simply failed to listen.

The lesson of the *War of the Worlds* fiasco is that we hear mostly what we want to hear, not necessarily what someone else is trying to tell us. And this occurs in serious negotiations as well. Consider what happened to an attorney friend of mine. He was representing a construction contractor who had spent substantial sums of money preparing for a huge job with a hotel chain. Unfortunately, the job had been awarded via an oral contract, and the hotel chain subsequently reneged on the agreement. When the contractor sued for reimbursement of his expenses, the hotel chain denied the existence of the oral contract. The contractor's attorney explained the problem to his client in explicit terms.

"Oral contracts are very difficult to prove," said the lawyer. "When you get up on the witness stand, you must be careful not to say anything that would raise doubts about the existence of the contract. Do you understand?"

"Yes," replied the contractor. "You've made it quite clear."

"We can't say anything that will damage our contention that an oral contract exists," said the lawyer again, reinforcing his point.

"I've got it," said the contractor. Unfortunately, he didn't— he was too busy thinking about the money he might lose to really listen to his lawyer's warning.

When the case came to trial, the attorney for the hotel chain questioned the contractor on the witness stand.

"When did you enter into the contract?" asked the hotel attorney.

"Well," said the contractor, "we didn't actually have a contract per se!"

As the contractor's lawyer had feared, the judge threw the case out.

Many conflicts can be resolved easily if we learn how to listen. The problem is that we are often so busy making sure that people hear what we have to say that we forget to listen.

I hate to admit it, but I used to be a poor listener. Getting my point across was more important to me than listening. When I left the Marine Corps, a company called Dun & Bradstreet, which had just computerized its entire database, hired me to sell credit information to other companies to use for marketing purposes.

My sales territory was the Canal Street area in New York— then considered the armpit of Manhattan Island. This was the toughest place to sell door-to-door, which is what I was being paid to do. My employer trained me to make a strong sales pitch, but it proved ineffective, so I experimented with another approach—keeping my mouth shut and listening to what people had to say. I learned very quickly that this was the key to success in selling.

I discovered that my sales prospects would tell me everything I needed to know in order to make the sale *if* I just kept quiet long enough. If I tried to make a verbose, flowery presentation, I would be thrown out. But if I let them talk to me instead, they would buy anything.

In the years that followed, I came to the realization that this approach is also the key to successful negotiating, and that *trust* is a necessary ingredient for a successful negotiation. But how do human beings create an atmosphere of trust? By listening. Human nature is to trust people who really pay attention to what we have to say. Unfortunately, few people are good listeners. Too many negotiations fail because the parties are not really listening to each other. In fact, according to leadership guru Barry Wishner, "The number one reason why change does not take hold in Corporate America is the inability of leaders to listen."

But listening is not a difficult art to master. In fact, it's quite simple. It's similar to keeping physically fit: The hard part is getting to the gym on a regular basis, but once you're there, it's easy to do all the exercises.

With listening, the hard part—"getting to the gym"—is shutting up. But if you can train yourself to keep your mouth shut most of the time, it's easy to be a great listener, and a great negotiator.

Developing the Desire to Listen

Ironically, most of us think that communication is telling others what we think and what we want. We assume that they will hear us and then do what we ask them to. We are so inwardly focused, so narcissistic, that all we seem to think about is "us." We forget to include the other person in the equation.

Many years ago I was having lunch at a bistro in St. Paul de Vence, a picturesque hill town in the south of France. In my fractured French, I tried to order a bottle of beer.

"Je voudrais une bouteille de bière, s'il vous plaît." I would like a bottle of beer, I told the waitress.

"In a can," she replied.

"No," said I, "En bouteille!" In a bottle.

With her hands on her hips and a sneer on her face, she repeated, "In a can!"

Now I was really getting mad. "Not in a can," I insisted. "In a bottle. En bouteille. *En bouteille!*"

She threw her hands up in despair. "Monsieur, *in a can!*"

"All right," I said. "Have it your way. Give it to me in a can. Anything. Just give me a beer!"

She stormed off and returned with a bottle of Heineken. "Heineken," when you say it in French, loses the "H" and sounds like "in a can." I practically fell off my chair I was laughing so hard. I realized I had been so myopically focused on my own needs that I simply forgot to include her point of view in the equation.

Let me ask you a simple question: Do you trust a person who does not pay attention to what you think and feel? The reason for most failed business deals and failed relationships is that somebody isn't listening. Listening to others can be the most effective item in your negotiation toolkit. If you give the other person the opportunity, he will tell you everything you need to know. And he will like you more as well. We like people who listen to us.

The 70/30 Rule

The most important rule for being a good listener is: *Always let the other person do most of the talking*. This is a simple matter of mathematics. I call it the *70/30 Rule*: Listen 70 percent of the time and talk 30 percent of the time.

This is revolutionary in our culture because we have been taught just the opposite. In years of English classes, we are taught to express ourselves, orally and in writing. We are told that successful people are people who can get their ideas across, and that it is important to express not only our ideas, but our feelings as well. No one impressed upon us the importance of listening, much less taught us how to do it.

If you want to change all that, you must reverse the order of things. Instead of doing most of the talking, do most of the listening. Just shut up! It works. And the best part is the effect it has on the other person. We all love people who are willing to listen to us talk about our favorite subject, ourselves. From now on, think of yourself as a detective whose job is to extract information from other people. Let them talk.

Don't Interrupt

Your attempt to listen can be thwarted by the temptation to interrupt the other person to tell him something you think is vitally important. It isn't, so don't. When you are about to interrupt, ask yourself if it is really necessary. Instead of adding to the conversation, your interruption may end it prematurely.

A few years ago my television broke down. I decided that it was time to buy a new one. So I went to the local appliance store, Circuit City, and decided to purchase a beautiful 27-inch Sony TV. I had always heard that Sony made an excellent product. As I reached into my wallet for a credit card to pay, a salesperson came over.

"Can I help you?" he asked.

"Yes," I replied. "I'm interested in that 27-inch Sony. I've always wanted to have one and . . ." Before I could finish the sentence, he cut me off.

"Are you sure you want a Sony?" he asked.

"What?"

"We have two other units that are much better," he said, probably thinking he could sell me a more expensive set. "We have a Panasonic over here, and right there is a Proscan that sells very well." He proceeded to explain why these other TVs were superior to the Sony. By the time he finished his spiel, I was confused.

"Maybe I better think about it," I said as I left the store. The next day I decided to have my old TV repaired. I never purchased the Sony, or any other new TV. If the Circuit City salesman had refrained from interrupting me, he would have made a substantial sale. I suspect that salespeople who are unable to resist the temptation to interrupt buyers (who have already decided to make a purchase) cost companies millions of dollars of lost sales each year.

Listen Actively

It's not enough just to listen to someone—you want to be sure that they *know* you are listening. *Active listening* is the art of letting the other person know that you're hearing their every word. Although you may be capable of multi-tasking (doing the *New York Times* crossword puzzle while listening to someone, for example), the person speaking may take offense at your divided attention and assume you really don't care about what she has to say.

One technique of active listening is asking questions. Questions prove that you are following the other person's train of thought. It is impossible to ask questions if you are not listening. More on asking questions in a minute.

Eye contact is another important part of active listening. Have you ever been engaged in a conversation with a person who was scanning the room looking for the "important" people? Did you feel abandoned? When speaking to such a person, the feeling of being ignored is almost unavoidable. They never look you in the eye. Yet if you told them you felt this way, they would say, "Keep talking, I'm listening."

Eye contact is important, but it doesn't need to be overdone. You don't have to lock eyeballs for the entire time the person is talking. This makes people uncomfortable. You should, however, make enough eye contact from time to time so that they can see you are with them.

Your body language also should indicate that you are paying attention. Keep your body facing the other person and try not to fold your arms, as this may suggest that you are not receptive to what that person is saying.

Listen for Nonverbal Messages: Body Language

Studies show that as much as 90 percent of communication is nonverbal. Much of this is via body language. To be a good listener, you need to decode these messages.

Most of us are not adept at picking up body language. In *The Man Who Mistook His Wife for a Hat,* neurologist Oliver Sachs describes how victims of brain damage often will compensate for lost cerebral functions by developing other abilities to a remarkable degree. Some of Sachs's patients, whose neurological damage prevented them from understanding spoken language, were able to pick up subtleties of body language that were not perceived by people without brain damage. Sachs recalls how a group of these patients broke out into uncontrollable laughter while watching a politician speaking on television, because the speaker's body language sent the message: *I'm a liar.* To these patients, it was obvious from the politician's body language that he was being insincere. The rest of the public missed the clues.

The best way to sharpen your ability to read body language is by practicing making observations and analyzing the results. For example, let's say you are conducting a business meeting in a room where the temperature is cool. You notice that the person you are negotiating with is perspiring. What's wrong? People normally don't perspire in cold rooms. Is he nervous? If so, maybe there is more going on in your negotiation than meets the eye.

Paying close attention to facial muscles can be useful as well. If a person is squinting, frowning, or tightening around his mouth, he may be holding something back. In a case like this, I always ask, "Is something troubling you?"

Posture is another good clue as well. If the other person is seated, is he leaning toward you, or is he leaning back in his chair? If they are interested in what you are saying, their body language will be open and leaning in your direction.

Make it a habit to observe the nonverbal behaviors of your negotiation partners. It will pay dividends.

The Interviewer's Art: Asking Questions

What if the other person doesn't feel like talking? That is where the art of asking questions comes into play. Questions get people talking. Think of yourself as an interviewer— Barbara Walters, or my personal favorite, Detective Columbo. They listen *and* question. So should you. Here are some tips for asking questions that will further your negotiation:

Open-Ended Questions

Open-ended questions are those that can't be answered with a simple yes or no.

"How could we do this?"

"What do you think about that idea?"

"How do you feel about that suggestion?"

The opposite is the closed-ended question, which can be answered with a simple yes or a no. It leaves you with little more information than you had when you began.

To answer an open-ended question, the other person must give the question some thought and then provide a detailed response. Remember, your objective is to get the other party to talk more, in order to encourage her to offer up as much information as possible. Open-ended questions encourage the other person to talk about her needs, desires, fears, strategies, and so on.

Of all the strategies I have learned in several decades as a negotiator, this is probably the most potent: People are more likely to do what I want them to when given the opportunity to talk about themselves. Recently, I was attempting to convince the president of a consulting firm to hire me as the keynote speaker for their annual meeting.

"I am considering several other speakers," he said to me. "Why should I hire you over them?"

Instead of becoming defensive and selling my qualifications, I asked him a series of open-ended questions about his company and his meeting.

"What is the purpose of your meeting?"

"What do you want me, as your keynote speaker, to contribute to your meeting?"

"What have you liked or disliked about speakers you've hired in past years?"

The answers to these questions dragged on for fifteen or twenty minutes each. My interviewer wanted to answer these questions. He felt safe knowing that we were dealing with his issues and not mine. He became so caught up in telling me about his concerns and needs that he forgot that I hadn't been hired yet.

After about an hour, he said, "I guess we ought to cut you a check. How much do you need?"

I hadn't asked for the order. The open-ended questions had made him comfortable and so it just seemed natural that I be hired. I told him my fee and he wrote me a check on the spot.

Don't Put Others on the Defensive

Questions that suggest a person's motives or thinking are not sound may put him on the defensive and cause him to clam up. For example, simply asking "Why?" can be intimidating. When you ask an employee, "Why did you do that?"

she may think that you disapprove of her actions, and rush to defend rather than explain them.

Instead of asking, "Why do you feel that way?" ask "How come you feel that way?" or "What makes you feel that way?"

It's a subtle distinction, but an important one. If I ask you, "Why do you feel this way?" you may interpret my question as an attack, or a value judgment. What you may hear is, "You must be out of your mind to feel this way." Using the more neutral "how come" softens the impact of the question. It is no longer a challenge, it's just a simple question.

This is true not only in business negotiations, but in personal ones as well. In dealing with teenagers or children, try this. Ask them, "Why did you do such-and-such?" You'll find they will automatically go on the defensive and clam up. In their minds, you have just attacked them, whether you intended to or not. On the other hand, if you say, "What made you decide to do such-and-such?" your question is no longer perceived as an attack, but as an attempt to understand their behavior. The difference in their response will amaze you.

Ask for Advice

Another way to demonstrate your listening skills and impress the person you are negotiating with is to ask for her advice or opinion. "What would you suggest we do to resolve this?" Everyone loves to be asked for advice. It boosts the ego. When someone asks for my advice, I feel smart, important, and respected.

One subtle way of asking for advice is to use the phrase "What if?"

"What if we did it this way?" "What if we tried that?" After posing the question, give the other person a chance to express his views.

Offering alternatives is a similar technique. Asking, "Which option would you prefer?" demonstrates your respect for the other person and his opinion.

And of course you can always ask about the other person's feelings. People love to have their feelings validated.

Many years ago I applied for the job of sales manager at a computer company. The vice president of the firm, who was making the hiring decision, would not give me a definitive answer, so I decided to be proactive.

"I believe that I am a terrific candidate for this job," I told him. "But I don't know how you feel. Could you give me some advice on what I should do to convince you?"

Upon hearing me ask for his advice, he softened his demeanor and opened up.

"Actually, we like you very much," he said. "Our problem is that we can't offer you a position for another month."

Aha! I had discovered his reason for hesitating. When I agreed to wait for a month, they hired me.

Ask for Clarification if Needed

Considering that many negotiations fail because of misunderstandings, it makes sense to seek clarification whenever you don't completely understand what the other person is trying to say. Most of the time we don't bother to do this and instead make assumptions about what *we think* the person is trying to say. Those assumptions are often wrong.

I witnessed a remarkable example of misunderstanding when I worked for IBM. Two sales managers were noisily arguing about which selling strategy to employ for a prospective client. Because we worked in an open bullpen environment, at least fifty people witnessed the disturbance.

"We must recommend two 370 computers," insisted the first manager. "One for each of their main locations."

"You are completely wrong about this," replied the second manager. "What we ought to do is . . ."

Each manager was convinced that his strategy was the best one for the account. The shouting and posturing went on for at least twenty minutes. The two men became so angry at each other, the bystanders were sure a fistfight was imminent.

Suddenly one manager said, "Wait a minute! I'm talking about Client X."

"What?" said the other. "I'm talking about Client Y."

The entire battle was fought because of a simple misunderstanding as to which account they were strategizing.

An excellent way to prevent misunderstandings and convince someone that you really are listening is to repeat back what was said.

"Let me be sure I understand what you're saying. You're saying that Client X should have two separate computer systems?" In other words, regurgitate what *you believe* was said. You might even consider repeating what was said *incorrectly*. This technique will give him an opportunity to correct you, which will make him feel even more important.

Asking for clarification is always an excellent way to clear up needless misunderstandings.

Being a Detective

Well, I've given you the basics on listening. Now all you need to do is practice. If you want to see an incredibly effective listener in action, turn on a rerun of a *Columbo* episode. I advise all my negotiators to think of themselves as detectives—they know how to listen carefully and actively—and no one is better at asking probing, open-ended questions.

WEEK THREE

Strengthen Your Negotiating Position

Never contend with a man who has nothing to lose.

—BALTASAR GRACIÁN

A recurring frustration I overhear from my training program participants is, "I can't get anywhere when I negotiate because the other side holds all the cards. I have no power. The other side has no reason to give in to my demands." How you perceive the strength of your position is an important consideration when you negotiate. If the other side does indeed hold all the cards, it would seem that you are in a difficult position.

The good news is that negotiation power is a state of mind. It comes from:

a. Having options.

b. Being able to demonstrate to the other party that they will be hurt by not agreeing.

c. Convincing the other party that although they have options other than those you are proposing, you're both better off making a deal.

Negotiation power is subjective. You are powerful or powerless depending on how you perceive your situation. In other words, *you are in a powerful position if you believe you are.* Power in negotiation is really a matter of self-confidence. If you convey self-confidence to others, they'll perceive you as being powerful. In most cases, the person who says, "The other person holds all the cards" is just lacking in confidence. By refusing to acknowledge the strength of his own negotiating position, he is actually giving his negotiating power away.

Week Three will address the sources of your negotiating power so that you will not be intimidated by a seemingly more powerful opponent.

Limits to an Opponent's Strength

While working as sales manager for a large computer manufacturer, I reported to a national sales manager who, in my eyes, was psychotic. He regularly threatened his subordinates, took clandestine photos with a spy camera, carried a handgun, and unsuccessfully tried to coerce my secretary to provide evidence that I was incompetent. The other managers who worked for this man felt powerless in the face of his abusive behavior. But I refused to accept that I was powerless. I asked myself: *What are the limits to his power?* He may have a gun, I thought, but he can't shoot me. (At least not without going to jail.) He can only fire me. I knew that I had more power than others realized. So I presented my case to the general manager of our division, demonstrating my total commitment to the company and my colleagues by placing my job on the line.

"Here are the facts," I said. "This man is costing the company an enormous sum of money by demotivating the entire sales force. Either you fire him, or you can fire me right now."

My gamble paid off and the manager was fired.

Successful negotiators see the glass as half full. They are optimists, and they are confident. They believe they are powerful and downplay the threat posed by the other side.

When assessing a powerful adversary, the average person will magnify the other side's strengths and minimize its weaknesses. Our tendency is to focus on our own deficiencies. But for effective negotiators, the telescope is reversed. They focus on the other negotiator's flaws and weaknesses rather than their own.

Finding Their Hot Button

The key question in every negotiation is: What is the pressure on the other person to make this deal?

When you focus on your own limitations, you miss the big picture. You may as well give up. If you are negotiating with a Donald Trump, the question is not, "How can I convince him to do what I want when he is so important?" The question is, "What does he stand to lose if he does not make this deal?" Trump may have a lot of resources at his disposal, but his power is still limited by his need or desire to come to an agreement.

Your negotiation power derives in part from the pressures on the other person. Even if she appears nonchalant during the negotiation, she inevitably has certain worries and concerns. It's your job to be a detective and root these out. If Trump is committed to building a fifty-story office/co-op building and you own a small portion of the land, what is the pressure on him? What happens if the project falls apart because he fails to obtain your 50-by-100-foot lot? You are in the driver's seat—not because you have more resources than Trump, but because of the pressure he is under. He has more at stake because you could undermine his ability to complete the project.

There is a story, an apocryphal one perhaps, that Trump once needed to buy a piece of property that was key to a building project in New Jersey. He made the owner an offer and gave him twenty minutes to come up with an answer. "If you don't agree after twenty minutes," Trump reportedly said, "I'm going to shelve the entire project and you will get nothing." The owner folded under the pressure and agreed to Trump's terms. I don't know if this story is true. (Would Trump really scrap a major real estate project just because one property owner got tough in negotiating for his lot?) If it is true, I have to applaud Trump for using Brodow's Law: Always be willing to walk away. Had the owner in this story realized Trump's precarious position and called his bluff, the selling price for the property would undoubtedly have gone up.

If you discover that the other side is under pressure, look for ways to exploit that pressure in order to achieve a better result for yourself.

Commitment: Demonstrating Your Convictions

Good negotiators test each other to determine the extent of the other side's commitment to its position. In my experience, most people are rarely so committed to their position that they are willing to walk away if the other side will not agree to their terms. If you have the courage to stick to your guns, your opponent will be forced to conclude that you have been pushed to your limit and that it is time to concede. For this reason, the Ultimatum can be an important part of your arsenal. When you give someone an Ultimatum—"This is my final position and I am not budging"—you are sending a powerful message about your intentions. (See Week Eight for more on the Ultimatum.) The more committed you are, the more powerful your negotiating position is.

Another source of negotiating power lies in getting the other side to commit to the negotiation. For example, a smart seller will always try to get the buyer to agree that he loves the seller's product so that he will be more committed to making a deal. If you can convince the other negotiator to expend a lot of time and effort in the negotiation, his stake in reaching an agreement will be greater. The higher his stake, the more difficult it will be for him to walk away, and the more likely he will be to offer you concessions.

The Confidence Mystique

In a previous book, *Beating the Success Trap,* I shared my observation that many people seem to subscribe to a *victim mentality*: By unwittingly allowing themselves to be used, hoodwinked, and exploited by others, they give away their negotiating strength and position. My solution is what I call the *Confidence Mystique*. If you give signals that you are in charge, that you know what you're doing, you are less likely to be victimized.

The full power of the Confidence Mystique impressed itself upon me when I tried to get fired from a sales management job I hated. I tried a myriad of ways to "persuade" my superiors to fire me. I was outspoken and obnoxious, late for work, argumentative in meetings, and prone to taking long lunches from which I often did not return. Unfortunately, my strategy backfired. The employers interpreted my brassy attitude as a superhuman level of confidence in myself that, by their reasoning, must reflect superhuman abilities. Instead of firing me, they offered me two promotions, one right after another and each with an accompanying pay raise. Then something even more extraordinary happened. My division was sold to another company and 1,500 salespeople and managers were let go. Only six remained, and I was one of them! They sensed confidence and, despite my irresponsible behavior, they found it so irresistible they couldn't bring themselves to let me go.

People bow to confidence. What is behind the self-assuredness is secondary to the impression it makes.

Know Your Options

One of the prime reasons we tend to give in more often than we should is that we don't fully understand the options that are available to us. If you are afraid that you have no alternatives, you will probably act rashly. When I tore the cartilege in my knee, for example, my surgeon wanted to operate immediately.

"What if I don't have the surgery?" I asked him.

"Your knee could lock up, leaving you unable to walk," he replied.

That sounded like a frightening possibility. I called on old buddy who is an orthopedic surgeon. "He's trying to scare you," my friend advised, "so you will agree to the surgery. In reality, your condition may not affect your day-to-day activities."

My fear disappeared and I was able to consider my options, one of which was to walk away—literally, in this case—from having the surgery. And so I did.

As I suggested in Week One, your willingness to walk away is one of the most potent sources of your negotiating strength. That willingness is based upon your perception that you have options—alternatives to making the deal. (The professors at Harvard call this your BATNA: Best Alternative To a Negotiated Agreement. I call it having options. Go figure.)

Patience and Persistence

It is frightening how impatient people in our culture can be. But if you can recognize someone else's impatience, you can use it to your advantage. When you sense that someone is in a hurry to complete a negotiation, you can take the advantage simply by taking your time.

Our impatience often stems from our fear that if we don't agree quickly, the deal will evaporate into thin air. That may be true in some isolated instances, but most of the time it is not. When you start to feel impatient, take a deep breath, and let the other person be anxious instead. Whoever is more flexible about time has the advantage.

Knowledge

"Knowledge is power." The more information you have about the people with whom you are negotiating, the stronger you will be. Collect information whenever you can. Without it, you can find yourself out of the game. (See Week Four to learn what kind of information to collect.)

Risk-Taking

Most people will do anything to avoid taking a risk. But risk avoidance is death to investors and to negotiators. I am a staunch believer in the adage, "Nothing ventured, nothing gained." The key is to take reasonable risks based upon reliable information. One good question to ask yourself is, "If I take a risk and it fails to pay off, what is my fallback position?" (Review Week One for more on risk-taking.)

Legitimacy

According to *Webster's New World Dictionary,* something is legitimate when it is sanctioned by the authority provided by law or custom. We bow to authority. You are powerful in a negotiation when your position is supported by authority.

Here are some types of legitimacy you can call upon:

1. *Anything in writing has automatic legitimacy.* As we saw in Week One, people are intimidated by contracts simply because they are in writing. Have you ever found yourself afraid to challenge a statement contained in a

contract? In law school I learned a simple technique for contract negotiation that has been worth its weight in gold. Whenever you disagree with a clause in a contract, simply cross it out, write in your own version, and initial it. Now the statement in writing is yours. And if the other party doesn't object to your change, it becomes part of the agreement.

2. *If a practice is the norm in your industry, it has legitimacy.* For example, in the residential real estate industry, 6 percent is the normal commission for the sale of a house. Because it has legitimacy, few buyers or sellers will contest it.

3. *If something is your company's policy, it has legitimacy.* When a hotel charges me for free 800 calls, I ask the desk clerk to remove the charge from my bill. The response is often: "I'm sorry, we can't do that. It is against our company policy." Most hotel guests will accept that response. (My rebuttal is: "Paying for free telephone calls is against *my* company's policy.")

4. *Precedent has legitimacy.* Precedents are difficult to dislodge. Why do you suppose that credit card companies, phone companies, newspapers, and other businesses try to get you to sign up for long-term contracts? To lock you in. When it comes time to renew, the chances are very high that you will do what you did the last time.

5. *Expert opinions have legitimacy.* Why did the United States attack Iraq? The experts at the CIA said that Saddam Hussein was developing "weapons of mass destruction." We often listen to the experts without verifying their conclusions. If you can support your negotiating position with expert testimony, you are in a position of strength.

Weakness as Strength

A young seminar participant said to me, "Ed, I am intimidated by the people I am required to negotiate with, all of whom are older and much more experienced than I am. What can I do?"

"Use it," I replied.

"How can I use it?" he asked. "It is my weakness."

He failed to realize that weakness can be a source of strength if you use it properly. I advised him to admit to his "opponents" that he is inexperienced and to ask them for their help and guidance.

"I really don't understand this. Can you help me?"

As we've discussed, people are often flattered, and therefore more receptive to your position, when they are asked for advice.

Being the weaker of the two opponents can sometimes be used to your advantage. One of my favorite Peter Sellers movies is *The Mouse That Roared.* Sellers plays the wily prime minister of Grand Fenwick, a tiny European duchy that declares war on the United States. He recognizes that the U.S. does not want to be perceived as a bully, so he decides to lose the war so he can receive American foreign aid. The next time you are in a seemingly powerless position, throw yourself on the mercy of the court and ask for its help. Like Peter Sellers, you may lose the battle but come out ahead anyway.

Detective Columbo is adept at this approach. He loves to play dumb. Instead of showing people how smart you are, allow others to demonstrate how smart *they* are. Let them come up with the answers. Most people love to show off. Let them, and then use it to your advantage.

WEEK FOUR

Preparing to Negotiate

If you don't know where you are going, you will probably end up somewhere else.

—LAWRENCE J. PETER

Now that you feel confident that you are negotiating from a position of strength, you are ready to prepare to actually negotiate. Here are some of the things you should be thinking about.

SETTING TARGETS

Having high aspirations is fine, but it also helps to set specific targets. Three types of targets provide a road map for your upcoming negotiation.

Target Number One: Maximum Position

The *maximum position* is the best you could possibly do in the negotiation. For example, in a salary negotiation, what is the absolute most your employer will pay? If you know the company is prepared to pay as much as $100,000, you would be doing yourself a major disservice by asking for only $75,000. In order to open the negotiation with an extreme position (See Week Seven), you must have a sense of what the maximum position is.

Target Number Two: Your Goal

Your goal in a negotiation is the result you will be satisfied with. This is not necessarily what you would like to have (for we all *want* to achieve the maximum position, no matter how much of a long shot it may be), but what you will be content with. In some cases, you will not want to settle for anything less than the maximum, but most of the time your goal will realistically be something lower. For example, if your house is for sale at $250,000, which is the maximum, but you will be satisfied if it sells for $220,000, then $220,000 is your goal. You might be willing to settle for less than your goal, but only under pressure.

Target Number Three: Your Bottom Line (Minimum)

Your Bottom Line is the worst outcome you will accept under pressure. You may not be totally satisfied with the Bottom Line, but it is preferable to walking away. Once you know your bottom line, you won't be goaded or tricked into an unacceptable outcome. If your house is offered at $250,000 and your goal is to get $220,000, your bottom line may be $200,000, which is what you will accept if the house has not sold after three months. For anything less than $200,000, you'll refuse to sell, and the house will stay on the market.

STARTING POINT

A major question in every negotiation is, "Where should I open?" This will depend upon the nature of the relationship you enjoy with the other person. If there is a high level of trust, you may want to skip the formalities and open with your goal. Place your cards on the table. If the relationship is adversarial, or you do not know the other negotiator very well, you probably will want to start closer to your maximum position and leave yourself more room to negotiate. (See Week Seven on Concession Making and opening with an Extreme Position.)

CONCESSION LISTS

Before entering a negotiation, make two lists of concessions—one of those you are willing to make, and one of those you are not. Prioritize your concessions by deciding which you'll make first. Make a third list of minor concessions—concessions you will make but that will not cost very much. Knowing in advance what you will and won't agree to will prevent you from giving up too much during the heat of the discussions.

STRENGTHS OF YOUR POSITION

Make a list of the strong points of your position. This will give you confidence and help you decide what to highlight during the negotiation. If you are selling your house, consider:

- All the benefits that the buyer will receive. Does the house have a big backyard? A jacuzzi in the master bedroom? Is it located in a good school district? These will all strengthen your position.
- The dynamics of the market. Is it a seller's market? Have you received many offers? This too will bolster your position.
- Your deadline in selling the house. Do you have one? If not, this is also a strength, as it affords you the flexibility of holding out for the best offer.

DEADLINES

Deadlines can affect the balance of power in a negotiation. Are there any deadlines? If so, who created them? If you created them, can you change them? If the other side created them, can they be challenged? The danger of deadlines is that you are more likely to make mistakes at the last minute, and most deals are consummated at the last minute. So most mistakes are made under the pressure of a deadline. Can you impose a deadline on the other side? If you can, good for you. But don't allow the other negotiator to impose a deadline that you aren't comfortable with.

INFORMATION ABOUT THE OTHER PARTY

The best time to begin collecting information about the other side is as far in advance as possible. The other party will be more relaxed about sharing information with you before the negotiation begins.

Where can you get your information?

- First, the other negotiators. Ask them—they might tell you what you want to know.
- Someone else in their organization. A secretary, or a colleague. They may not be directly involved in the negotiation (or even know about it), so they are more likely to divulge information that will help you strengthen your position.
- A third party who has had prior dealings with your opponent.
- Published information. It never hurts to research the other party prior to the negotiation. "Google" them; so much information can be found online today.

Their Pressure

The most important question you can ask yourself is, "What pressures exist on the part of your opposing party?" A person under pressure is more likely to make concessions.

Their Targets

Now you have to find out what will satisfy the other side. What are their goals? They may be closer to yours than you think.

Position versus Needs

If you are myopically focused on the other side's position, you may never reach agreement. Look beyond their position to what is really motivating them in the negotiation. Once you understand how they think, you can seek options for mutual satisfaction.

A classic example is a sales negotiation in which the buyer raises price objections. This is usually a smoke screen. Price is rarely a deal-breaker. The major criterion in a buying decision is: Will this product/service solve our problem? Price may be an important consideration, but usually it is number three or four on the list.

The vice president of a Fortune 100 company called to invite me to be the keynote speaker for an upcoming convention. He stated his position in no uncertain terms.

"We don't have that much in our budget," he said after I quoted my fee.

Instead of allowing myself to fall for his trap, I diverted the conversation to what I believe is the number one concern of all my clients: Will the speaker bring something of value to the meeting? After we discussed how my qualifications, experience, and speech content were a good match for his meeting, this client agreed that I was his number one choice. Once he had acknowledged the value I brought to the table, the fee became a mere technicality, and he hired me at my full fee. The fee issue was just his *position*. His real *need* was to find the best speaker for his meeting—me.

THE AGENDA

The agenda is a list of all the items that are to be discussed in the negotiation. You should always have an agenda ready when you go to the negotiating table. To reach a satisfactory agreement, three questions should be addressed:

1. *Have we identified all the pertinent issues?* If you don't identify important items in advance, you may forget them later on. Having a written agenda going into the negotiation will ensure that you remember to deal with the things that are important to you.

2. *Does the agenda reflect your priorities?* Which issues are most important to you? Which do you want to deal with first? Sometimes you are better off saving the more difficult issues for last. (See Rule Number Three in Week Six.) How much time do you want to spend on each issue? Are any issues outside the scope of this agreement?

3. *Does the agenda favor your position?* If possible, it is best to be the author of the agenda. As the author, you can slant it in favor of your own interests. If the other side writes the agenda, be prepared to challenge their priorities. Don't feel obligated to begin where they want to begin, or to devote time to issues that you believe are not relevant. If the agenda does not include points of importance to you, be assertive and add the items *you* want to discuss.

LOCATION: WHERE TO NEGOTIATE?

The location you choose for the negotiation can affect the outcome. It's always nice if the location is comfortable and convenient for you, but it's more important that it be appropriate and reflect your strategic interests.

Advantages of the Home Court

Holding the negotiation on your turf offers the following advantages:

- You have access to your facilities and decision makers. For example, you can call upon senior management if high-level decisions are required. Additional information is also at hand, and experts can be produced on a moment's notice.
- You have more control over the other negotiators. You can arrange the layout of the meeting room according to your preferences. The other side will find it more difficult to arrange interruptions or distractions if you have positioned them strategically.
- Negotiating on home territory can be psychologically advantageous. You will feel more comfortable and confident; and confidence, as we have discussed, is power.

Advantages of Negotiating on the Other Side's Turf

- When you are asked for concessions that you are not prepared to give, you can claim limited authority. The absence of senior management can be a good excuse for refusing certain terms of the agreement.

- You have access to the decision makers on the other side, and can try to influence them.
- You have access to noncombatants, i.e., people who are not directly involved with the negotiation. These people—secretaries, engineers, and other support personnel—can provide information that will enhance your position.
- Your opponent will feel more relaxed and therefore more willing to consider your point of view.

Advantages of a Neutral Zone

The formality of most business venues can have a constricting effect on the participants. Getting away from the office to a more congenial atmosphere, such as a restaurant, golf course, or tennis court, can foster candid exchanges of information. During my corporate sales career, one large deal continued to elude me because I was unable to create quality time in front of the busy decision maker. Eventually I lured him to lunch at his favorite eatery. No interruptions. No phone calls. We had a delightful meal followed by an easy close. Happy (and well-fed) people are easier to persuade.

INDIVIDUAL OR TEAM?

One important decision you have to make is whether to enter the negotiation alone or with partners. Here are the advantages of each approach:

Advantages of Going It Alone

- *Decisions can be made more quickly.* Working with your negotiation partners can be even more time-consuming than negotiating with the other side. Before you begin a negotiation, you must first negotiate with your partners over all of the points to be discussed. What is our position on each issue? Where should we begin? What concessions should we make? And so on. This process is not only time-consuming, it can lead to an internal deadlock if teammates disagree.
- *You avoid weakening your position due to differences of opinion among the team members.* Rest assured, even within a team, differences will crop up. The other side may even try to create discord among your team members. They will certainly attempt to take advantage of your squabbling.
- *As an individual, you can claim limited authority as the reason for refusing a concession.* In a team situation, limited authority is more difficult to justify—one of your partners may possess the elusive authority, or you may hold it collectively.

Advantage of Going in as a Team

- *Teams can avoid the pitfall of making hasty decisions.* If one team member is about to make a mistake by agreeing too quickly, another member can stop her. Individuals tend to be in a hurry. Teams tend to be more patient.
- *Two heads are better than one.* In a team, you have the

benefit of hearing other people's ideas and opinions. Each person can make a contribution based upon his unique qualifications.

- *You can bring in experts.* Having experts on your team will raise your credibility and legitimacy.
- *There is strength in numbers.* This is true in two ways. First, the other side will be affected psychologically when you present a united team. Groups are more intimidating than individuals. Second, you will be more confident in your position if you have partners to back you up.
- *The individual experiences less pressure in a team environment.* When your partner does the talking, you have more time to listen and to think. And when you are negotiating as a group, you can diffuse responsibility for the outcome.

REHEARSAL

As a former professional actor, I am a staunch believer in the value of rehearsals. Though a negotiation often relies more upon improvisation than memorization, the benefits of rehearsing are significant. A negotiation can be rehearsed by role-playing—just ask a colleague to assume the role of the person with whom you will be negotiating. Rehearsing will help you:

- *Develop your own strategies and tactics.* Through practice, you will discover the approach that feels most comfortable for you.
- *Understand the other side.* The other negotiator's po-

sitions and interests will be clearer as your rehearsal partner acts out his role.

- *Anticipate the other side's gambits.* While role-playing, you will get a preview of the strategies and tactics the other side may use.

WEEK FIVE

Traditional Strategies: Win-Lose

I aim high, and then I just keep pushing and pushing and pushing to get what I'm after.

—DONALD TRUMP

Traditionally, Western negotiation has emphasized getting what you want at the expense of the other person. In Week Seven we will examine how both sides can get what they want—a process known as win-win negotiating. But first we need to understand how most people have been taught to think when they negotiate. You cannot really master "win-win" until you understand traditional "win-lose" strategies. Many negotiators will use them, so you should know how they work.

OPENING GAMBITS

Traditional opening strategies emphasize keeping your cards close to the vest while learning as much as you can about the other party.

Aim High

Donald Trump says that aiming high is the main thrust of his negotiating strategy. This is one point on which The Donald and I are in accord. When you aim high, there is always the possibility that you will achieve the maximum. By aiming for more than what you will be satisfied with, you can make concessions and still hit your goal. Nothing is more demoralizing than aiming low and settling for a mediocre outcome, then discovering that the other side was desperate to make the deal and would have done better.

During another sort of boot camp—the one run by the Marine Corps—I once had trouble jumping over a large ditch while carrying a rifle and seventy pounds of gear on my back. I was gauging my jump by aiming for the far edge, but wound up in the ditch every time. Then one of my buddies gave me some excellent advice.

"Aim beyond the ditch," he said.

So I focused on a point well beyond the ditch and I made it.

Aiming beyond the ditch works in negotiation as well. A friend in Carmel, California, applied this principle when she bought her oceanfront home. At the time, the house was on the market for $2 million. She offered $1.2 million, figuring she had everything to gain and nothing to lose. It paid off. The seller accepted.

Let Them Open First

This adage is based on common sense. If you allow your opponents to make the first move in a negotiation, they may surprise you with low aspirations. A buyer may offer more than the seller was expecting, or a seller may ask for less than the buyer was willing to pay. Conversely, if you open first, you may leave money on the table by offering too much or asking for too little.

Keep Your Mouth Shut

Traditional negotiators subscribe to the theory that you are better off not sharing information with the other side. This makes sense in an adversarial negotiation, because your opponent will use it to obtain concessions from you. (In a cooperative negotiation, information is used to achieve mutual satisfaction.) While lying in a negotiation is unethical, withholding critical information about your pressure to make the deal is not.

I learned the value of withholding information at the age of nine. My friend and I were innocently walking through Prospect Park in Brooklyn when we were accosted by a gang of tough-looking older kids.

"Where are your parents?" asked the leader of the gang.

I was about to answer honestly that they were at home five miles away. Fortunately, my friend was more attuned to the situation than I was.

"Our parents are right over there," my friend said as he pointed vaguely in the direction of where we lived.

He didn't lie, but he revealed the very minimum amount of information. And it was a darn good thing he did, because had we shared the truth, we would undoubtedly have been beaten up and robbed. And that is exactly what could happen to you in an adversarial negotiation. For example, if you are a buyer, and you reveal to the vendor the extent of your budget, his price may expand accordingly. Tight lips are a virtue.

MIDDLE GAMBITS

Managing Expectations

Everything you say and do will affect what the other side expects to get out of the negotiation. When you send the message that you need the deal badly, you raise the other party's expectations, causing them to be tougher and give up less. If you send the message that you don't need to make the deal, their expectations will be lowered and they will be more open to making concessions.

You can see this principle in action at a car dealership. A buyer who says, "I need a new car because the old one just broke down" automatically raises the salesperson's expectations. The price of the new car will undoubtedly go up. But a buyer who tells the salesperson, "I have a car just like this at home but I'm thinking of buying a second one for my husband," will lower the salesperson's expectations (and therefore the price), because he will realize that the buyer can easily change her mind about buying a second car if the price isn't right.

So always be careful not to raise the other side's expectations.

Creating Satisfaction

Satisfaction, after all, is the ultimate goal in every negotiation. You want to do everything you can to satisfy the other party, to let them feel that their needs have been addressed. However, this does not mean that you have to give in to their every demand. Here are five ways to create a satisfied opponent without giving away the store:

1. *Offer a Meaningful Explanation*

If you can offer someone a good reason to accept your position, he will be assured that you are not taking advantage of him. You want the other negotiator to say, "I don't like this, but I can understand why it makes sense." When my plumber charges me an arm and a leg to fix the toilet, he justifies it by showing me his company's pricing book—remember the power of legitimacy—and I accept it because I realize that all its customers, not just me, are paying this price.

This applies on a personal level as well. Let's say you have to negotiate your teenager's allowance. He insists that he needs an increase so he can afford to keep up with the other kids at school by purchasing "cool" clothing, a particular (and expensive) brand of athletic shoes, and a new, high-tech cell phone. Instead of just saying, "Sorry, your allowance stays as it is," you explain to him that because money is tight, you can't give him the increase until you have paid off his substantial dental bills. Since you made the effort to give him a good explanation, it will be easier for him to understand and appreciate your decision, and he will realize that you still care for him.

2. Give a Minor Concession

Some negotiators need to feel as if they have won something in the negotiation. It doesn't matter what, as long as they think they've convinced you to give something up. When dealing with such a person, give her a minor concession—something that means more to her than it does to you. We all place different values on concessions, so something that doesn't cost you a lot can be really meaningful to them. For example, in a salary negotiation with a subordinate, you may be unable to give him the raise he wants. Instead, offer him a new title and a bigger office. This doesn't cost you a thing, but your employee will still feel as though he has won something.

3. Stroke Their Ego

People love to be complimented. If you can't give a substantial concession, lavish your opponent with praise. If you can't give that employee a raise, or a new title or a better office, at least tell her how much her work is appreciated. She may value the validation even more than a raise.

4. Present an Ultimatum

"This is the best I can do, take it or leave it." When you give the other party this ultimatum, they realize that they have pushed you to your limit. In other words, they have done the best they could in the negotiation. This gives them a sense of satisfaction. (See Week Eight for more on the Ultimatum.)

5. *Listen to Them*

We all crave attention. Satisfaction can be derived from knowing that the other person is really listening. One of my favorite examples is described by actor Kirk Douglas in his autobiography *The Ragman's Son*. As a boy, Douglas writes, his father ignored him most of the time. So one evening, when he threw the contents of a scalding cup of tea in his father's face, his father picked him up and threw him across the room. Amazingly, Douglas claims it was one of the happiest moments in his childhood because his father had finally paid attention to him. Businesspeople, too, crave attention. Give them the opportunity to speak; they'll get satisfaction out of the mere fact that you listened.

The Use of Time

Time becomes critical when one or both of the negotiating parties have deadlines. In our culture, it is more than likely that someone will be in a hurry. From the outset, the side without the deadline has an advantage over the side chasing the clock. As I will explain in Week Eight, buyers typically use the delay tactic, while sellers try to create a deadline or sense of urgency for the buyer.

Caucus

Failure to listen is not the only common shortcoming in a negotiation. People also don't take time to think. Making snap decisions in the heat of negotiation can turn out to be disastrous. That is why it is useful to have a *caucus*. The caucus is simply a break in the formal negotiation. It may be an hour, an entire day, or a month. It is simply a way of stepping back and taking time to think before entering into an agreement.

When you have a team of negotiators, the caucus is almost mandatory. As the negotiation progresses, each member of your team will form a different opinion. Each person will hear different things and develop different conclusions about what your strategy ought to be. The only effective way to keep the team on the same page is to hold periodic caucuses. In fact, the caucus can be longer than the negotiation session that preceded it.

Even when negotiating alone, it can be useful to take breaks to get some clarity. Tell the other side that you need to use the restroom, make a phone call, or grab a bite to eat.

Any excuse will do. Just go. It is an opportunity to clear your head and think.

CLOSING GAMBITS

Walking Away

Again, being willing to walk away can foster a favorable outcome in and of itself. Here's how.

1. *Walking away may force the other side to soften their position.*

I once received a call from the president of an East Coast high-tech company.

"I'm looking for a keynote speaker for my upcoming conference," he said. "You were recommended. You have three minutes to tell me why I should hire you!"

Something about his brusque manner irritated me. I decided not to do business with him.

"Actually," I replied, "I'm very busy right now, and I don't think I'm the right speaker for your group anyway. You better find someone else."

He quickly went from curt to pleading.

"What do you mean?" he said. "You have an excellent reputation. Why won't you speak for us?"

My willingness to turn him away broke down his obnoxious attitude. I was hired—without having to justify my qualifications or put up with this man's rude behavior.

2. *Your willingness to walk away demonstrates your commitment.*

Savvy negotiators are always testing you to see how committed you are to your position. In order to convince them, you may have to resort to strong measures—including walking out.

3. *Walking away can help them sell your position to their boss.*

They may have to justify their concessions to someone higher up on the food chain. Now they can tell the boss, "See, we had to make those concessions or they would have walked away from the deal." Buyers need to justify a greater expenditure, and sellers must have a good reason for lowering their price.

Breaking an Impasse

Some deals should simply never happen. But even in situations where we want to make a deal, we can find ourselves stuck in an impasse. Here are ten tips for avoiding deadlock:

1. *Change your negotiator(s).*

A common cause of deadlock is the negotiators' failure to get along. You should not feel bad if this happens to you. We are human beings, and we often experience emotional reactions to other people. The best way to fix this is to admit the problem and get someone else to step in for you. The new negotiator won't have the negative history with the other side and will be able to relate to them in a more constructive way.

2. *Change the level of the negotiation (up or down).*

If you are dealing with someone who has no authority to make decisions, you are negotiating with the wrong person and should find someone further up the chain of command. If you are a customer in a store, or a potential buyer at a car dealership, ask to speak to the manager. Conversely, in many negotiations, for example with a Japanese company, you may find it easier to negotiate with a middle-level executive rather than with a CEO or vice president.

3. *Change the location of the negotiation.*

Sometimes the formality of a business setting may create a rigid, stuffy atmosphere. This is especially true if the negotiation is being recorded. Switching to more comfortable quarters—a restaurant, the golf course, a ball game—can loosen things up. Going "off record" helps the other persons to reveal their bottom line, if they were not comfortable doing so back at the office. In some countries, most negotiating takes place off the record. (See Week Eleven.)

4. *Change the structure of the agreement.*

By changing the terms or length of the agreement, you may break through whatever obstacle was holding up the deal. The car dealer does that when he suggests financing a car over a five-year period instead of paying up front—

paying $500 a month is easier than paying $25,000 all at once.

5. *Take a break.*

When tempers flare, negotiations can go downhill fast. As we have discussed, one good strategy is to take a break. Invoke a "caucus," or a recess. Or suggest quitting for the day and resuming the next morning, when everyone will be refreshed and will have forgotten what they were so angry about the day before.

6. *Introduce new information.*

Bringing in new information can tip the scales toward making a deal. It can also help the other side save face. A software company recently contacted me to tell me about an upgrade to a product that had previously been inadequate for my needs. The new information about its product convinced me to buy it.

7. *Confront the obstacle.*

By simply asking what the problem is, you may discover that the negotiation is being sidetracked by something you hadn't thought of. Once you understand the problem, you can find the solution. If you can, ask off the record—they are more likely to tell you.

8. *Offer alternatives: Ask "What if?"*

Negotiators often have tunnel vision. They become stuck in one mode of thinking. By offering alternative solutions— "What if we did it this way?"—you may open their minds to possibilities they hadn't considered.

9. *Make minor concessions.*

As I've stated previously, many deadlocked negotiations have been resolved because someone offered a minor concession. This can be especially true when you are dealing with a Tough Guy, who has decided not to make the deal unless he receives a concession from you. Offering a minor concession can break that impasse.

10. *Switch from combative to cooperative problem-solving.*

Many negotiations fail because the emphasis is on winning. This can create a lot of bad feeling and preclude an agreement that would be in both sides' interest. The antidote is switching from adversarial to cooperative negotiating, from Win-Lose to Win-Win. Show the other side that you understand their needs and that you are committed to finding a solution that meets them. I'll discuss this in detail in Week Seven.

WEEK SIX

Concessions Make the World Go Round

To please people is a great step toward persuading them.
—LORD CHESTERFIELD

Negotiation is all about give-and-take. Concessions are an integral part of the negotiating process. Ironically, *what* you give up is not as important as *how* you give it up.

Recently I participated in a negotiation that made use of both adversarial and cooperative techniques. For thirty years I have played a game known as four-wall handball. Handball and its sibling, racquetball, are played in an enclosed court, forty feet long by twenty feet wide. Sadly, fewer and fewer new players are being introduced to these sports, which are dying out. As a result, many health clubs are converting their courts to aerobics and weight-training areas. My health club offers the only remaining handball/racquetball courts in the local vicinity. When I joined the club twelve years ago, we had six courts. Ten years ago, new management converted two into weight rooms. Last month, another new owner bought the club and informed us that the four remaining courts were going to be converted into exercise and weight areas.

The handball and racquetball players, about fifty in all, were up in arms. Where would we go to play? We had supported this health club for years. How could the new owner threaten to do such a dastardly thing? A group of about thirty of us met with the new owner, who gave us a chance to air our grievances and open a dialogue. His position was that he would make more money by using the handball courts for exercise and weight areas, since the club has 3,000 members, and only 50 of them use the courts. He suggested we do the math.

We rebutted with the following:

1. The ballplayers form the nucleus of those people who actually use the club, which amounts to a small percentage of the total membership. (Most people sign up but never show up.)
2. As the only health club in the area with ball courts, our club enjoys a certain prestige that attracts new members, even though most of them may never actually use the courts.
3. If other underutilized areas of the club are used for the expansion of exercise and weight areas instead, then the ball courts can be left alone and everyone will be happy.

After the ballplayers had their say, the owner announced that he had decided to keep at least two of the ball courts, and possibly a third, depending on the feasibility of using another underutilized area of the club for his weight-training room. The ballplayers were delighted. We had managed to save at least two courts, which was infinitely better than none.

I was not privy to the owner's thinking, but I can surmise that his original announcement to close down all four courts may have been an example of aiming high, an attempt (conscious or not) to lower the expectations of the ballplayers. But the owner was also an excellent listener. He gave us a chance to express our options for mutual satisfaction. After a period of discussion, he gave in by agreeing to keep at least two courts. Holding out the possibility of retaining a third court was an excellent way to bring us down slowly. We ultimately lost the third court, but by even considering keeping it, he created the impression that he was listening to us and trying his best. And that satisfied most of the ballplayers.

Think about this: What if the owner had stated his original position as, "I'm taking out two of the four courts"? Would the ballplayers have been satisfied with the final result? I doubt it. The ballplayers would still have presented their arguments, but it wouldn't have saved any of the courts. We would have ended up with the same number of courts, but would not have felt as though he had made any concessions or that we had influenced his final decision. The result would have been identical, but we would not have experienced satisfaction.

On the other side of the coin, the ballplayers were smart to band together. Had it not been thirty of us versus one owner, we might have lost all four courts. It seemed to many in the group that individually we had no power, but thirty handball/racquetball players acting as a united front must have been intimidating to the new owner.

Remember my original point: The ballplayers were satisfied not because of what the owner gave away, but because of *how he did it*. In many negotiations, the concessions do not satisfy the party on the receiving end. They get what they wanted, but—because of the way the concessions were made—*they walk away feeling dissatisfied*. The following rules for concession making are designed so that each concession you give results in maximum satisfaction.

Open with an Extreme Position

I make this a rule for most negotiations: *Ask for a better outcome than you are willing to settle for.* Sellers should ask for more than they want, and buyers should offer less than they are willing to pay. Again, this is basic psychology. Opening with an extreme position leaves you room to give something away. The other side feels satisfied when it can obtain a concession from you. When you open with an extreme position, you can enjoy three benefits:

1. You will lower the other side's aspirations. The announcement that all four handball courts were being converted to weight-training areas lowered our expectation of saving all four courts. (Note: If you do not open with an extreme position, you may *raise* the other side's expectations.)
2. You have room to give the other negotiators a concession, which helps them feel satisfied.
3. They may surprise you by accepting the extreme position.

This means that you don't have to agree to the other negotiators' opening position. It is likely that they have also opened with an extreme position and allowed room for movement.

Let's say I am selling my house at an advertised price of $300,000. If you offer me anything close to my asking price, $290,000 for example, I will think that you have a lot more to spend. You have raised my expectations. I will kick myself because I didn't ask for $350,000 instead of $300,000. So even if I receive my full asking price, I may still be dissatisfied. "I should have asked for more!"

Now, suppose your first offer is only $240,000—an extreme position relative to the $300,000 listing. I may abandon my hope of getting the asking price of $300,000. If we eventually settle at a price of $258,000, I will feel good because I succeeded in getting you to move up from $240,000. Think about this: I will be more satisfied with $258,000 than I would have been in the first scenario with $300,000. Why? Because of *how* you made your concessions.

Looking at this negotiation from the seller's point of view, suppose the seller was hoping for a sale at $250,000. By opening at $300,000, the seller receives more than $250,000 and the buyers can still tell their friends that they "stole" the house for $258,000. If the seller had been hoping to actually sell the house for $300,000, the asking price should have been $325,000 or $350,000. (Caution: If your position is too extreme, you may drive all potential suitors away.)

Let me give you an example involving an airplane manufacturer. Let's say the estimated delivery date for a new airplane is twelve months. If the manufacturer were to announce a twelve-month turnaround, an anxious customer would probably insist on ten months. So using the principle of the extreme position, the manufacturer leaves room to negotiate by telling the customer that the airplane will be delivered in eighteen months. Hopeful for an early delivery, the customer negotiates this down to fourteen months. The customer is happy because he thinks he has saved four months and the manufacturer has not only avoided sabotaging its twelve-month delivery schedule, but has actually gained two more months.

Next question: *How extreme should your opening position be?* Answer: As long as you can provide *reasonable justification,* no position is too extreme. How can you justify an extreme position? Here's an example of how a real estate buyer can justify a low opening offer on a house:

- This is all we can afford.
- The house needs work.
- Comparable homes on the street have sold for less.
- The school system isn't as well regarded as those in neighboring communities.

If you open with an extreme position without offering justification, the other side may conclude that you are not dealing in good faith and walk away from the table. But when you do give reasonable justification, the other side may say, "I am not thrilled with this, but I can understand why they did it."

Make Small Concessions

Large concessions imply weakness and desperation. It makes sense. Why would you offer a large concession if you were confident about your negotiating position? You wouldn't. If you make a sizable concession, it may lower your opponent's perception of your value. Say you are about to hire a graphic designer. She quotes her fee as $100 an hour.

"What!" You flinch. "That's awfully high."

"Okay," she says. "I'm not too backed up right now, I guess I could do it for $50 an hour."

What is your reaction? *If she is any good, why is she offering to cut her fee in half? Maybe she isn't as good as I thought. Should I hire someone else?*

Mercedes-Benz, for example, refuses to offer large price concessions on its vehicles. They know that the perceived value of their automobiles will be more if they stick to their sticker price. The resale price of their cars remains higher as well—a plus for Mercedes-Benz owners. Refusing to make major concessions convinces the buyer that he has pushed the seller as far as he will go. The same is true in reverse. If the buyer only makes a small concession, the seller may well conclude that the buyer has reached the limits of her budget.

Vary the Size of Concessions

If every concession you make is the same size, you are encouraging the other negotiator to ask for more. Instead, each concession should be less than the one before it.

Let's return to the example of buying a house. The buyer offers $240,000 against the seller's listed price of $300,000. The seller drops the price to $290,000, which the buyer rejects. So the seller comes down to $280,000, followed by another drop to $270,000. The buyer observes that each time the seller's offer is rejected, the seller drops the price by $10,000. The buyer recognizes the seller's pattern, and expects the seller to drop another $10,000.

Instead, the seller could make an initial concession of $10,000 (to $290,000), followed by $5,000 (to $285,000), and then $2,000 (to $283,000). The buyer will eventually get the message that the seller's bottom line is somewhere in the low $280s, and the buyer will likely be satisfied that a price around $280,000 represents the best possible deal.

Don't Make the First Move

As I mentioned in Week Five, you should always allow the other negotiator to make the first move. Her opening move could be a lot less aggressive than you thought it would be if it turns out that she has low aspirations and is anxious to make the deal. If you had opened first, you might not have discovered this.

Suppose you are negotiating for a raise. Instead of saying, "I want a $10,000 raise," ask your boss, "How much can you offer me?" He may offer $15,000. Then you can ask for $20,000, whereas if you had asked for $10,000, he may have offered only $5,000.

Never Accept the First Offer

If you accept the first offer, the other side will feel they left money on the table.

"We could have done better," they will think. "It was too easy."

You are hoping to sell your house for $250,000. Your asking price is $300,000. A buyer offers $270,000, which is

$20,000 more than your goal. You are ecstatic. "We better take it before they disappear." So you accept the offer. What happens to the buyer? "We must have offered too much," the buyer concludes, and decides to withdraw the offer.

Let's try it again. The buyer offers $270,000. You reject the offer. The buyer offers $275,000, which you also reject. They come back with $278,000, which you accept. You are delighted to receive $28,000 more than your goal of $250,000. The buyer is satisfied because he feels he pushed you to your bottom line.

You Don't Have to Make Reciprocal Concessions

You are not obligated to respond to a concession by making a concession of the same value. If the home-seller drops the price from $300,000 to $290,000, the buyer is not obligated to go from $250,000 to $260,000. You don't have to match the other side dollar for dollar.

Make Straw Demands

Many negotiators flood a negotiation with a long list of demands. In all likelihood they do not expect to win all of them. Their strategy is to throw as much as they can against the wall and hope that some of it will stick. A straw demand is one that you do not particularly care about and do not expect to win. In the end, you can trade it for something you do want.

Suppose the next time you purchase a new car, you want an upgraded sound system. You can set up a straw demand by asking for a set of upgraded wheels (that you don't really care about). When the car dealer balks at giving you the wheels, tell her that you will relinquish that demand if she throws in the upgraded sound system.

To counter a straw demand, learn as much as you can about the other side's real needs. When you have done your homework, it is easier to cut through the "straw" so you can focus on what they really want. We'll talk more about straw demands in Week Eight.

Claim Limited Authority

How often have you asked sales clerks in a department store, "Can you give me a discount?" How often have they replied, "I'm sorry, I don't have the authority to do that"? And—here's the tough one—how often have you said, "Okay. Never mind. I'll take it."

Claiming limited authority is such a useful tactic because most people don't have the time, inclination, or wherewithal to challenge it.

Offer Peripheral Concessions

Instead of offering a concession in price, try sweetening the deal by throwing something extra into the package. Some years ago I was hesitating about whether to buy a new car. The dealership had come down several thousand dollars from the sticker, but it was still $200 over my target price. The sales manager broke the deadlock by offering me a $300 add-on at no cost: Armor All, a product that comes in a bottle of goo and protects the paint and the body of your vehicle. It probably costs the dealer $4.95, but it was listed on its price sheet as a $300 option, so I felt that I was getting an additional concession that was worth $300. I bought the car. Before entering your next negotiation, make a list of the nonmonetary concessions you can offer. Or if you're on the receiving end, think of those you would accept if you fall short of your target.

Splitting the Difference

Most of the books and articles I have read about negotiation say, "Whatever you do, NEVER split the difference!" I tend to shy away from absolutes. But I will tell you that when you offer to split the difference, *you are conceding half the difference!* A smart negotiator will hold out for the other half.

Going back to our real estate example, say the home-seller has come down from $300,000 to $280,000, and the buyer has come up from $250,000 to $260,000. At this point, someone—the seller's real estate agent, perhaps—will say, "Why don't we split the difference and settle at $270,000?" Okay, I know what you're thinking: "Sounds like a compromise, what's wrong with that?" What's wrong is that the buyer may respond, "No. Why don't we split the difference of the difference and settle at $265,000?" The seller has, in effect, agreed to come down from $280,000 to $270,000 *without even realizing it.*

So be careful when you have the opportunity to split the difference. However, here is one situation in which I believe it makes sense: You have won every point in the negotiation. The other side is practically bleeding and they simply can't give any more. Suddenly they say, "Why don't we just split the difference?" In this case, it may make sense because it is a chance for you to give the other side some satisfaction. They can save face. Let them win this battle; you already won the war.

Getting Something in Return

Whenever you give something away, always get something in return. Another way of saying this is, never make unilateral concessions. If you do, it is as though you are negotiating against yourself. When you give something away without requiring the other side to match it, they will feel they are entitled to your concession, and won't be satisfied until you give up even more.

So the next time you make a concession, tie a string to it: "I will do this *if* you do that." And make it clear that if they don't agree to do *that,* you are not obligated to do *this.*

People are more likely to do something for you when you have done something for them. Psychologically, the best time to request a concession is right after you have given one.

Make Them Work for Concessions

When I was a boy, a generous uncle would often stuff a few bucks in my pocket, but he always made his gift contingent upon my doing the dishes, which he knew I hated. He wanted to teach me a lesson, and it was a valuable one. We tend to have greater appreciation for the things we earn than for the things we are given.

A Realtor friend was representing the seller of a residence.

"Should we fix the roof before putting the house up for sale?" the owner asked my friend.

"No," he replied. "If you do it in advance, it will be taken for granted. Let the buyers ask for it. Then they will feel that they won something."

When people get something for nothing, they appreciate it less, and they may be inclined to ask for more. When someone asks you for a concession, make them earn it.

Leave Something Small on the Table

When you are winning the negotiation handily, it makes sense to leave a little something on the table. Let the other side go away with the feeling that they won something, too. You'll let them save face, and they'll remember that next time you're at the negotiating table together.

Don't Get Carried Away

Now that you are aware of the rules for concession making, let me finish Week Six with a warning: Rules are made to be broken. The rules for concession making will work most of the time, but it is prudent to allow for exceptions. Each individual negotiation must be analyzed on its merits. My friend Jerry found this out when he tried to sell his old washing machine.

Jerry and his wife, Betsy, had just purchased a new washer and dryer. But the old washer still had some life left, so they decided to sell it. They had originally paid $500 for it, ten years earlier. Betsy wanted to place an ad in the local newspaper offering the old washer for $100. Jerry, however, fancied himself a savvy negotiator.

"We're going to get three hundred for it," he assured Betsy.

"That's too much," she replied. "A hundred dollars would be fine."

"Now honey," said Jerry (who must have been following the advice I've outlined here in Week Six), "you have to understand how negotiation works. If we offer it for sale at $100, someone will offer us $50. After some haggling, we might wind up with $60 or $70. But if we advertise it at $350, we'll get an offer of $250 or $300, maybe even more."

"Are you sure?" Betsy asked.

"Trust me," was his response.

They placed the ad the following Monday: "Brand-name washing machine. Excellent condition. $350."

On Monday they received no calls. The same was true for Tuesday, Wednesday, and Thursday. Jerry and Betsy began to get nervous. Finally, on Friday, a prospective buyer called.

"Can my wife and I come by to look at the washing machine?"

At eight that evening a young couple arrived, examined the machine, and went outside to talk it over in private.

"We like it," said the young husband as the couple returned from their deliberations. "But we just got married. The best we can offer is $200."

I guess Jerry was right, Betsy thought. *We asked for more, and we're going to get more!*

Betsy was about to say, "We'll take it" when Jerry jumped in and told the couple, "I'm so sorry. We have another buyer coming over at 8:30. If you want the washer, you'll have to pay the asking price of $350." Jerry, of course, was bluffing.

The newlyweds decided to have another conference.

"I think we should have taken the $200," said Betsy.

"They offered us $200," Jerry advised. "It's obvious that they want it. They will come up with at least another fifty, maybe more."

At that moment Jerry and Betsy heard a car starting up. Looking out the window, they watched in shock as the young couple and their $200 drove off down the street.

No one else answered the ad.

This occurred about five years ago. Whenever I stop by, Jerry shows me the old machine. Betsy insisted that it should occupy a special place of honor in their garage to remind Jerry in case he ever decides to show off his negotiating skills again.

Jerry says that some day he will donate the old washing machine to the Smithsonian and take a tax write-off.

The Three Rules for Win-Win Negotiating

It isn't that they can't see the solution. It is that they can't see the problem.

—G. K. CHESTERTON

THE BAR ASSOCIATION AND THE GODDESS OF DISCORD

In the typical adversarial negotiation, both parties behave as though the other side is the enemy. This only serves to create an atmosphere of distrust. Here is an example:

Mr. X was smack in the middle of a lawsuit when he hired me as a consultant. His company had patented a new safety process for its industry and a competitor had allegedly stolen it. He was suing the competitor for patent infringement. Initially Mr. X retained a major West Coast law firm. These lawyers advised him that the defendant was prepared to go to trial.

But a full year later the suit had yet to go to trial. It had become so convoluted that Mr. X was having trouble communicating with his lawyers and had to retain an independent attorney to act as liaison with the big law firm. In other words, Mr. X hired a new lawyer to talk to the other lawyers he had hired. The defending company was having a similar problem, so it also hired an independent attorney to act as go-between.

Six months later Mr. X discovered that he was having trouble communicating with the attorney who was hired to communicate with the big law firm. Are you following this? By the time I was hired to clean up the mess, both sides had spent more than $4 million on legal fees, with no end in sight. The attorneys had created such a complicated web of paperwork that no one knew what was going on. It was, of course, in the best interest of the lawyers—who were being paid at an exorbitant hourly rate—to amplify an atmosphere of discord and postpone a settlement for as long as possible.

After examining the facts, I was convinced that the defendant was ready to settle the case out of court. At my insistence, Mr. X called the liaison attorney and asked if he agreed with my conclusion.

"As a matter of fact," said the attorney, "I received a call two weeks ago from their attorney. Perhaps they do want to settle."

Well, thanks a lot. He hadn't bothered to inform Mr. X of the defendant's probe. Once we managed to get the two sides talking directly, without the interference of the lawyers, they were able to work out an agreement. If only they hadn't had such an adversarial attitude, and had agreed to sit down together at the beginning, they would have saved themselves two and a half years of worry and $5 million.

This sort of thing has been going on for thousands of years. In ancient Greek mythology, instead of attorneys, they had Eris, the Goddess of Discord. She is credited with starting the infamous Trojan War by creating dissension among the various Greek gods. Like it or not, Eris is still with us. Are your negotiations rife with discord? It's time you did something about it.

CHIMPS AND BONOBOS

Most people who attend my negotiation seminars tell me that they would rather go to the dentist than negotiate. Their reasons? Negotiation has been perceived almost exclusively as an adversarial activity: *you against me*. This perception exists because traditional negotiation is usually between two opponents who try to outduel each other. And at the finish, one party frequently comes out on top, and the other on the bottom. It is often referred to as "win-lose" negotiation, as in "I win and you lose." But there is a real danger to this dog-eat-dog style of negotiation. As celebrated sports agent Leigh Steinberg once said, "If you've got your foot on someone else's neck, at some point in the future, that person will have his foot on your neck."

So the traditional process of negotiation is flawed. When people treat each other badly, negotiations break down. The breakdown of diplomacy, which is a form of negotiation, often leads to war. And war, in this nuclear age, could lead to mutually assured destruction. No longer do we have the luxury of diplomatic deadlock. In world affairs, countries that have opposing goals often band together in pursuit of a higher good. We too must learn to regard other negotiators as allies rather than as enemies.

Unfortunately, our reliance on adversarial negotiating has made us distrust our negotiation opponents. We are haunted by the fear, "What if the other person takes advantage of me?" And in a sense, we are right to worry. Hostility has always been the mammalian way of responding to conflict. It would appear that adversarial behavior is in our genes.

Fortunately, one contrary piece of evolutionary evidence blasts such a theory right out of the water: *Bonobos*. Bonobos are a chimplike animal species of primate that live south of the Congo River in Africa. They are like chimpanzees that have attended finishing school: somewhat more elegant, sensitive, intelligent. Although bonobos share 98 percent of their genetic material with chimps (and humans), they differ from chimps in one significant area: The way they deal with conflict.

While chimpanzees are hostile, bonobos diffuse conflict by using their sexuality to keep the peace. Hostile emotions are kept in check by frequent lovemaking. The expression "Make love, not war" applies in a literal way to these clever (and frisky!) animals. Now don't get me wrong. I am not suggesting that humans should resolve conflict by having sex. I am merely pointing out that bonobos have discovered peaceful ways of getting along with each other. They remind us that we have a choice of how to behave when we interact. We can choose to be hostile and chimplike, or we can opt for a more peaceful, bonobo-like approach to settling our differences.

In Week Seven we will learn a bonobo-like style of negotiation: cooperative, or win-win, negotiation. *Win-win is a nonconfrontational method of negotiating in which the participants cooperate to reach an agreement that meets the needs of both parties.* Win-win enthusiasts say, "If the other side isn't happy, you haven't won." In fact, win-win negotiation is no longer about winning at all. It is about sharing, cooperation, and mutual understanding. It is about listening to each other's problems and caring about the results. Its focus is not on winning but rather on finding a mutually satisfactory solution.

THE THREE RULES

For more than a decade, in my Negotiation Boot Camp seminars, I have taught corporate executives three commonsense rules for applying this kinder, gentler approach to conflict resolution in all aspects of life. Here are my *Three Rules for Win-Win Negotiating:*

Rule Number 1: Change your behavior from adversarial to cooperative. Instead of accusing other people of being difficult, take responsibility for your own behavior and treat other people like partners. Even if they are unpleasant to deal with, don't imitate their rude or offensive behavior. Try to understand the source of their behavior and work to set a better example.

Rule Number 2: Develop trust by listening. We trust people who pay attention to our needs. Remember from Week Two that listening, the forgotten art, is the best technique for resolving a challenging negotiation.

Rule Number 3: Explore options for mutual satisfaction. If we put our heads together, we can arrive at a solution that addresses everybody's needs.

These rules aren't very complicated. They are just different from what we've been taught. Let's examine them in more detail.

RULE NUMBER 1: CHANGE YOUR BEHAVIOR FROM ADVERSARIAL TO COOPERATIVE.

It is not unusual for one party in a negotiation to declare, "The other side is impossible to deal with." We find it easier to blame the other person instead of admitting our own stubbornness. This kind of thinking gets us nowhere.

I have a different take on this. I believe that the only difficult person you ever really have to deal with is YOU! Psychologists tell us that we have no control over other people's behavior. The only thing we have control over is our own reaction. So the next time you are faced with hostile behavior, instead of allowing your primitive "fight" response to take over, overcome your own negative emotions. Change your behavior from adversarial to cooperative. Treat the other negotiator like a partner.

The most difficult obstacle in negotiating is overcoming your own negative emotions. So stop blaming other people and take responsibility for yourself.

A Classic Example

Elaine, a meeting planner in Chicago, was given the unpleasant assignment of putting together a retreat for two hundred senior executives in Hawaii with a small budget and only two weeks' notice. Elaine was a recent hire and felt under a lot of pressure to do a good job.

The first thing Elaine did was put in a call to a friend, who recommended a hotel on Maui.

"I've used this hotel a lot," her friend said. "The staff's very helpful and their rates are reasonable. Ask for Margie in sales. She's a doll. Tell her you're a friend of mine."

What neither Elaine nor her friend could have anticipated was that Margie was having the worst day of her life; her physician had just called with news that a spot had appeared on her right lung. Understandably, she was experiencing a lot of fear, anger, and denial.

When Margie received Elaine's request, she replied sarcastically, "You must be joking. Two weeks from now? For that budget? You must be crazy! The rates are high-season—and you can forget about discounting."

Elaine was shocked by Margie's rudeness. Instead of asking for her help, she responded in anger.

"I was told you were wonderful to deal with," Elaine said heatedly. "Can I speak with someone who understands common courtesy?"

Margie hung up, and that was the end of the negotiation. Margie lost the conference business and Elaine had to start from scratch.

Many negotiations fail because when we are faced with rude behavior, we respond in a hostile way. The negotiation is doomed before it gets off the ground. So the question is, how can we turn hostility into cooperation?

It is human nature to react defensively when confronted with hostility. Our brain consists of two main parts, the primitive stem and the more advanced cerebral cortex. The latter provides rational responses to external stimuli. However, the primitive stem usually reacts defensively to an attack before the rational mind has a chance to come into play. It was designed that way to protect us from predators. If a lion attacks you, it's not a good idea to take your time thinking about the possible alternatives. You must react immediately in order to survive. This has become known as the "fight or flight response."

When Elaine was verbally attacked by Margie, her primitive brain went into action and she struck back. Unfortunately, this was not an appropriate response for the situation—Margie is not a lion. The antidote to this kind of mutually destructive interaction is to give the rational mind a chance to intervene. When Margie responded sarcastically, Elaine could have curbed her defensive reaction and responded in a more thoughtful way. She could have simply ignored Margie's curt response and probed for the answers she needed. She had no control over Margie's demeanor, but she could have altered how she responded to it. If Elaine had taken a deep breath, ignored Margie's attitude, and treated her politely, Margie probably would have followed her example and a productive relationship might have ensued.

Overcome Your Negative Emotions

Don't mirror the other person's rude, stubborn, counterproductive behavior.

Using other people's behavior as an excuse for behaving badly is immature. When someone is rude and hostile, your feeling brain reacts by counterattacking. You get trapped into mirroring negative behavior, making an agreement impossible. Although you may be able to trust your emotional mind with some gut-level decisions like what to cook for dinner or what clothes to buy, you must give way to your rational, thinking mind if you want to turn a hostile negotiating opponent into a partner. In other words, you must transcend your own hostile reaction and change your behavior from adversarial—hostile, negative, closed—to cooperative. You must seek to understand the other person's behavior rather than imitate it. The only effective way to deal with "difficult" people is to learn how to control your own response to their negative behavior.

Focus on solving the problem.

You may recall from Week One that one of the Ten Traits of Successful Negotiators is the ability to focus on problem-solving. When you concentrate on solving the problem, the negotiation cannot be sabotaged by personalities or other irrelevant issues. If your objective is to be angry, then by all means focus on rude behaviors. But if your objective is to find a mutually acceptable agreement, then you must focus on finding a way to solve the problem. The best way I know to do this is to understand the reasons for the other negotiator's behavior.

Try to Understand Their Motivation

Don't try to beat them—try to understand them.

When people are rude and hostile, you have a choice of how to interpret their behavior. Don't assume the worst. Ask yourself, "What is causing their actions?" You may discover that they are being hostile because they don't understand all the issues or have all the facts. Or they may be reacting to something you did to offend them. Once you understand the source of their behavior, you can deal with it constructively.

Put yourself in their shoes.

Walk a mile in someone's shoes, the proverb says. When you approach the problem from the other side's perspective, you may experience a revelation. "Oh, now I get it. That's why they are so angry." We tend to look at the issues only from our own point of view instead of theirs.

Treat Them like a Partner

Lead by example.

Make it easier for the other negotiators to cooperate with you by setting a good example. If you act like an adversary, they will respond like one. If you treat them like an honored partner, they will reciprocate. This sets the tone for the entire negotiation.

Show respect.

Show respect for the people you are dealing with by treating them with dignity. Don't bruise their ego. Never insult or belittle them. Every person wants to be treated with respect. As we will see in Week Ten, this is the basis for what I call the Bonobo School of Management.

A Personal Example

One of my favorite examples of Rule Number 1 is the negotiation I had with my neighbor over the fence between our properties. One side of my living room is all glass, so one year I decided to extend the fence three feet, obscuring the view straight into my living room from my neighbor's house. However, I failed to notify my neighbor before doing so.

When my neighbor saw the addition to the fence, she angrily remarked, "What's the big idea? That fence ruins the whole look of my house!"

This was clearly absurd. My initial reaction was outrage. How dare she behave in such a selfish manner, begrudging me my well-deserved privacy over a measly three feet of fencing? Ruin the whole look of her house? That is an insult to my intelligence, I thought. But then I realized that she was just upset because I had not informed her in advance that I intended to extend the fence, which, after all, was on her property as well as mine. She didn't really care about the fencing, she cared about the principle. And now that what was done was done, what she was really after was an apology.

I made an on-the-spot decision not to react to her anger. Changing my behavior from adversarial to cooperative, I simply said, "I'm sorry. Just tell me what you want me to do, and I'll take care of it." She was so surprised by my conciliatory response that she dropped her complaint.

I had successfully resisted the temptation to mirror her rude behavior. Instead, I made the effort to understand her motivation and treated her with respect. It worked.

RULE NUMBER 2: DEVELOP TRUST BY LISTENING.

When I formulated the Three Rules for Win-Win Negotiating, I recognized the essential role that trust plays in the negotiation process. You will never enjoy a win-win relationship without mutual trust. Then I asked myself, how do you create this trust? So I thought about my own experience with regard to trust. And I realized, *trust comes from listening*. We trust people who pay attention to us, who listen to us. As a child, whom did you trust? Let me guess. Wasn't it the people who spent time with you, who listened to you? You knew these were the people who really cared about you. In adulthood, nothing has changed. We tend to trust people who listen to us.

Follow the 70/30 Rule

Take a moment to flip back to Week Two, when we discussed the 70/30 Rule—listen 70 percent of the time, speak only 30 percent. That rule should always be flashing in your negotiating mind-set. There is an entertaining story concerning nineteenth-century British prime ministers William Gladstone and Benjamin Disraeli. These famous men were the rock stars of their day. One lucky woman related her experience in dating both men.

"How would you compare them?" her curious lady friends inquired.

"Well," she said, "Mr. Gladstone took me to the theater. By the end of the evening, I was convinced that he was the most sophisticated, intelligent, and charming person in the world."

"And Disraeli?" asked one of her friends.

"There was a subtle difference," she replied. "Mr. Disraeli took me to the opera. By the end of the evening, I was sure that *I* was the most sophisticated, intelligent, and charming person in the world."

Listening can do all that and more.

Ask Questions to Clarify

Ask open-ended questions.

I wanted to hire a graphic designer to design a new brochure for my speaking business. The first three designers I interviewed wanted nothing more than to tell me how great they were and what impressive design projects they had worked on. The fourth designer opened our meeting by asking me an open-ended question.

"I understand you teach people how to negotiate," she said. "How do you do that?"

My reply took about fifteen minutes.

Then she asked, "What are you trying to accomplish with this new brochure?"

It took me twenty minutes to answer this question. By the end of the interview, I was convinced that she was the best graphic designer in the business. How come? She gained my trust by asking the right questions and listening to my answers. I did all the talking. She was hired.

Ask about their interests.

To obtain a clear understanding of people's needs, ask them. They may be totally surprised by your attention. If they have been acting cold and distant, this is a good way to break the ice and let them know you are seeking a win-win outcome.

Ask for their help in finding solutions.

Getting them to share ideas will create the impression that you want to work together, not against each other. Let them think the solution was their idea. When they feel connected to the outcome, they will be committed to reaching it.

Acknowledge Their Position

We have been taught to argue over positions. Your opponent states his position and you tell him why he is wrong. This leads to deadlock. A more productive way of communicating is to *acknowledge the other negotiator's position and then present your position as an addition, not a correction*. This happened to me recently when a potential client objected to my speaking fee.

"Your fee seems much too high," he said. Had he done his homework and checked out some other speakers, he would have discovered that my fee is reasonable.

"I can understand why you are taking this position," I said.

"You can?" he said with surprise.

By acknowledging his position, I was not agreeing with him. I was merely validating his right to differ. He was expecting an argument, and my unusual approach took the wind out of his sails.

"Certainly," I said. "If I were you, I would be concerned about how I spent my company's money."

"Thank you," he said.

"Let me explain how I look at this issue. You think I am being paid an exorbitant amount of money for a three-hour seminar. In reality, I will spend the better part of a week interviewing your employees, researching your business, and writing a customized negotiation role-play for your seminar attendees. In addition, traveling to and from your location will consume two more days."

"I never thought of it that way," he said. "Tell me some more about how you intend to customize the seminar for us."

The rest of the conversation had to do with everything but my fee. Once he understood the value of what he was getting, the fee was no longer an issue. He was able to accept my position because it was offered not as a rebuttal, but rather as a corollary to his. What I was saying was, "Maybe the truth lies somewhere in between our two positions. Try to look at it differently."

Woo Them

One danger in negotiation is that the other side will get the impression you really don't want to make a deal. You must convince the other negotiator that you truly want to work together.

I am constantly amazed at the differing behaviors of retail salespeople. Some act as though they could care less if I buy from them or not. I try not to do business with anyone who has that kind of "who cares" attitude. The seller who gives the impression "I'm so glad you are here" is the one who will earn my business. It is difficult to resist someone who appears genuinely interested in you and your interests.

List Common Interests

Another way to supplement your listening skills is to list the interests both of you have in common. The commonalities will become apparent when you take the time to focus on why the deal will be good for all concerned. Knowing that someone else shares your interests leads to trust.

Maintain Open Communication

A level of trust between the parties can erode when you fail to communicate regularly. Frequent meetings and conversations reinforce the impression that you are working together toward a common goal.

RULE NUMBER 3: EXPLORE OPTIONS FOR MUTUAL SATISFACTION.

Once you have successfully overcome your negative emotions, begun to treat the other side as a partner, learned to listen, and fostered an atmosphere of trust, you will be ready to choose a method for reaching an agreement.

Solve the Problem

Forgive me if I repeat myself on this issue, but it is critical. In order to be a win-win negotiator, you must set aside your ego and concentrate solely on reaching an agreement. When your goal is to reach an agreement rather than win at the expense of your opponent, the anxiety that used to accompany negotiation will disappear because the negative feelings associated with adversarial negotiation are eliminated.

Brainstorm Outcomes

The key benefit of a win-win approach is that both sides consciously collaborate on the outcome. Any agreement that is solely the product of one side is unsound. When both of you can claim authorship of the deal, it is more likely to last. The synergy that emerges from collaboration replaces the negative energy of the adversarial negotiation.

"What if we try this?" "What if we try that?" "How about . . . ?"

Do Research

Negotiations rarely take place in a vacuum. Most problems or issues have a history. So does the person with whom you are negotiating. Researching precedents is one aspect of the legal system that makes sense to me. How did someone else solve this problem? What interpretations of this issue have others conceived? Do I know anyone who has experience dealing with this person? When both parties to a hotly contested negotiation research what other people have done in similar situations, it can foster collaboration and agreement.

Ask an Expert

If you don't want to agree with me and I don't want to agree with you, why not bring in an expert and abide by his judgment? A builder once bought a vacant lot across the street from my house. When he announced his plans for the property, everyone on the block discovered that he intended to cut down a dozen beautiful trees. In my neighborhood we love our trees, and so we decided to take action. Our town has an Architectural Review Committee to prevent the area from being overdeveloped, so the neighbors petitioned the ARC to deny the builder permission to build on that lot. Arguments flew fast and furious from both sides. The ARC wisely dispatched the city forester, an expert in these matters. The forester determined that some of the trees were sick and dying, while others were healthy and could be expected to enjoy a long and fruitful life span. A deal was made in which the builder agreed to cut down only the sick trees. He hired a new architect, who drew up new plans for a house that would allow the healthy trees to remain. The neighbors were happy and the builder was able to finish his project—thanks to the expert.

Find Agreement

Wherever you can, find ways to agree. The more issues both sides can agree on, the more productive the negotiation will be. For that reason, I suggest beginning the negotiation with the easy issues and leaving the tough ones for last. If you begin with the most explosive issue, you may never get past it. You could deadlock right there. When you save it for the end, by which time you will have developed a positive relationship, neither side will want to see the relationship crumble because of one nasty issue, and it will be easier to reach a mutually satisfying solution. Your history of agreeing will motivate both of you to be more creative with the difficult portion of the negotiation.

Expand the Pie

Visualize a pie. It has a certain number of slices—let's say eight. When most people see the eight slices, they are trapped into believing that is the limit of the pie. But in reality, perhaps the solution is to bake a bigger pie.

Now let's translate the pie into a negotiation. You are in the electronics store trying to make a deal for a flat-screen television. The store is asking $3,000. You offer $2,500. The sales clerk rejects your offer. All he sees is the TV, his equivalent of the eight slices. But you envision a way to create four more slices. You offer to purchase a DVD player and a sound system for an additional $1,500 . . . if the store agrees to discount the price of the TV. You have just expanded the pie, which means that you have brought in *additional value from outside the negotiation.*

Expanding the pie is an excellent way to break a deadlock. When the scope of the negotiation is expanded and more is at stake, the players are forced to reevaluate their positions. Let's get back to my graphic designer, the one I wanted to hire because she knew how to listen. After I decided to hire her, we ran up against an obstacle: She was too expensive.

"Your fee is more than my budget," I informed her.

"I'm really good at what I do," she said. "I deserve to be paid well."

Neither of us would budge. It looked as if we were in a deadlock when she added, "Why do I have such a problem getting clients to pay my fees? They don't seem to care if I'm worth it or not."

Bingo! The lightbulb went on in my head. This was an opportunity to expand the pie.

"I have an idea," I said. "Corporations hire me to train their salespeople to sell their products and services at higher prices. If you will design my brochure at a special rate, I will show you how to get the fees you want."

"Ed, you must have been reading my mind," she said. "I've been thinking about hiring someone like you to coach me, but I didn't think I could afford it."

By expanding the pie to include my consulting services, both of us found satisfaction. I obtained a great brochure, and her income in the next year went up 30 percent, thanks to my coaching in sales negotiation.

WEEK EIGHT

Twenty Tactics to Die For

With foxes we must play the fox.

—THOMAS FULLER

You walk into a department store to buy a new dress. A sign informs you that the dress you want is "On Sale Today Only."

At the car dealer, the salesperson offers you a great deal. Then the manager walks in and says, "Oh no, we can't do that."

You are attempting to sell your product to a buyer who just can't seem to make up his mind. He keeps putting you off, week after week.

The prospective buyer for your house comes up with a list of thirty things you need to do before closing the deal.

These are examples of negotiation *tactics*. They are annoying, but they can be overcome. In most cases, if you can recognize what is going on, your awareness alone will disarm the tactic. Unfortunately, we often fail to recognize when someone is using a tactic against us. The way to prevent this from happening is to *understand* the kinds of tactics that a proficient negotiator has in his arsenal. Week Eight provides a rundown of twenty commonly used negotiation tactics, and my advice for how to deflect them when they are used against you as well as how to use them to gain an advantage over others.

1. The Flinch

The flinch probably deserves the award for the most frequently used negotiation tactic. You are negotiating with your boss for a raise. Your current salary is $50,000. You point out that you haven't had a cost-of-living increase in five years. You ask for $60,000, a $10,000 increase.

"What?" your boss responds incredulously.

You now feel like you are about two feet tall. *I must have been dreaming,* you think to yourself.

"Well, perhaps that *is* too much," you tell your boss. "What about $55,000?"

With a minimum of effort, your boss has just knocked five grand off your asking price—and the negotiation has just begun. The flinch works because it contains a hidden message: "Your behavior is outrageous, your request is so ridiculous that it doesn't even deserve a response, except to dismiss it completely." The impact of the flinch is emotional and nonverbal. You feel a tight sensation in the pit of your stomach.

Obviously my request was way too high.

Let's think about this tactic for a moment. Your boss is trying to get you to admit that your position is ridiculous. Why should you agree with him? There is no reason that I can think of. Here are some suggestions for *deflecting* the flinch:

- When your boss says, "You want how much?" you reply, "Should I have asked for more?" A humorous response like this sends the message, "It is your position that is ridiculous, not mine."
- You sit there with a straight face and say absolutely nothing. Now it's his turn to feel like he's two feet tall.
- You flinch back. "What!" you reply. "You don't think I am due for a raise? Don't you value my work?"

The important thing is to recognize a flinch when you see one. And don't be afraid to use the flinch yourself. When your doctor presents you with a bill for $350 for a simple consultation, exclaim, "What! $350?"

2. Emotional Barrage

You are conducting a performance review for one of your employees. Without warning, the employee starts yelling at you.

"Why am I always blamed for such things? I'm sick and tired of being treated this way!"

Like the flinch, the emotional barrage catches you in the gut. You weren't expecting a violent outburst. Feeling attacked, you attack back.

"Don't talk to me like that!" you might reply. "Who do you think you are talking to?"

And the situation goes downhill from there.

The emotional barrage can be intimidating. When the person we are negotiating with gets angry and seems to lose control, our first reaction is to mirror anger right back. Of course, this is counterproductive. Here is my three-step method for dealing with an emotional barrage:

Step 1: Give them a chance to vent their feelings. If you interrupt people while they are carried away by their emotions, or you try to argue with them, they will likely get even more upset, and both of you will lose. Instead, just listen. Once they have released their pent-up anger, they may be able to look at the real issue—solving the problem in the negotiation.

Step 2: Empathize with them, without agreeing. You can say, "I understand how you feel," or "That's unfortunate." Make calming sounds, for example, "Oh my," or "Oooo." It will help disarm the other party's outburst and prepare them to discuss the situation calmly and rationally.

Step 3: When they have calmed down, ask them what they really want. "What do you want to achieve?" or "What would you like me to do for you?" You may be surprised to discover that all they really wanted was to have their feelings validated. In terms of actual concessions, they may ask for very little. They may even apologize for their behavior and thank you for your tolerant reaction to the outburst. And if their demands turn out to be unacceptable, at least they will be able to discuss them now without shouting.

If all else fails, you may want to consider using the emotional barrage tactic yourself. Years ago, a friend of mine was up for the draft. He had a ruptured spinal disk that should have made military service impossible, but his condition did not show up in x-rays. He was having trouble convincing his draft board to declare him ineligible. Based upon my experience with the military, I advised my friend to use an emotional barrage in front of the draft board.

"Otherwise," I told him, "they may not believe you."

He took my advice, and his highly emotional defense of his physical condition was so convincing, he was ruled ineligible.

If you are unable to get what is rightfully yours by the usual means, you might consider using an emotional barrage. A little theatricality can be highly effective in a negotiation at the right time and in the right place.

3. The Sob Story

Your dentist has just presented you with an outrageous bill for your root canal. You don't want to tell him that you find his bill ridiculously high, so instead, you make a plea for sympathy by telling a sob story. "I just lost my job." "I have three kids in college." "My spouse just had open-heart surgery." "All I can afford is . . ." The dentist may feel sorry for you and agree to lower his rate.

The sob story works extremely well against a seller who is desperate to close a deal, or one who has inflated her asking price. An experienced buyer will use this tactic to test a seller's resolve. "I would love to do business with you, but I just lost a lot of money in the stock market and all I have in my budget is . . ." Many salespeople already believe that their own company's prices are excessive. Your sob story helps them to rationalize accepting a lower price.

If, on the other hand, you are on the receiving end of a sob story, here are some ways to deflect it:

- "Do you have any other budgets you can draw upon?" Perhaps the buyer neglected to tell you about his other resources.
- Call the buyer's bluff. She may be testing the legitimacy of your price. "I'm sorry, but I simply can't sell it to you for less."
- Offer alternatives. This is a typical approach a car salesperson uses when the buyer says, "I like this car, but I can't afford it." The dealer responds, "Then how about that less expensive model?" By offering an alternative, you will discover whether the buyer was telling the truth or not. He may say, "I don't want the less expensive model." Now you know that he wants the original offering and probably will find the money to pay for it.
- Change the payment terms. "Suppose you give us a down payment and pay the rest over a three-year period, or at the beginning of next year." This helps eliminate the obstacle when the buyer says, "I just can't afford this right now."

4. The Squeeze

Instead of saying, "I like your product, but I can't afford it," the buyer says, "I like your product, but I can buy it cheaper elsewhere." The squeeze draws upon the power of competition. By threatening to go elsewhere, you can compel the seller to offer a discount.

Here's how to deal with the squeeze if you are the seller:

- *Before offering a better deal, obtain more information about the competition.* A little research may reveal that the competitor's price is not in fact cheaper, or that its product is inferior. If you can pinpoint the buyer's hot buttons, you may find out that no one else's product does the job as well as yours. It also helps to find out what other offers the buyer has received.
- *Resell your product or service.* The key is to change the focus from "Who's got the best price?" to "Whose product does the best job?" In many cases the buyer does not understand what makes your product unique. This is often referred to as your Unique Value Proposition. As a seller, your job is to differentiate your product from the competition. By showing what your product does that the competitor's doesn't, you can justify the difference in price. If you can convince the buyer that your product solves his problem better than anything else, price becomes a mere technicality.
- *Tie a string.* If all else fails, agree to a discount only if the buyer agrees to do something for you in return. Ask the buyer to buy a larger quantity, or buy additional products, or agree to a longer-term contract.

There is a danger inherent in the squeeze. A seller who is compelled to give a large concession may decide to degrade the quality of the product in a subtle way that the buyer will have trouble detecting. Or the seller may pad his price to begin with, knowing that the buyer will demand a better deal. *Caveat emptor.* Let the buyer beware.

5. The Nibble

My bathroom floor was flooded. The plumber came over and found a leak in the washing machine line. He said he could fix it at a cost of $300.

"What?" I flinched. "$300! I can't afford that."

"What do you want me to do?" the plumber asked innocently.

I grimaced at the small lake in my bathroom and knew that I didn't have much choice. Once he was finished fixing the leak, I pounced with the nibble.

"While you're here, can you fix the funny noise in my toilet?" Since I had just paid him such a large sum for fixing the leak, I expected him to do this extra service at no additional cost, which he did. It made me feel a little better about the $300 charge.

The nibble is when one side asks the other for additional concessions after the deal is consummated. Buyers nibble by asking for free engineering assistance or additional product warranties after they have already purchased the product. Sellers nibble by requesting an extension of the delivery date. The nibble can benefit both parties. It creates customer goodwill and satisfaction, and it can make an exorbitant price seem less offensive, as in the case of my plumber.

But as a seller, if you are being nibbled constantly, it can be costly. If it is, here's how to respond:

- When the buyer asks for an additional free service, show him a price list. "Sure, we can do that, but here's what it will cost you."
- Just say no. The other negotiator may be testing you to see how much you are willing to give away. One way of doing this is to flinch by pretending that their request is a joke. "Fix that leak for free? Are you kidding?"
- Plead limited authority. "I wish I could do that, but I don't have the authority to give that away."
- Include the nibble in your price. If you are constantly being nibbled for a certain item, make it a regular part of the total package.
- Hold the other side to their agreement. "Sorry, your contract calls for a $20 charge if you are late with a payment." "We are depending upon your original delivery date."

6. Escalation

I once checked into a hotel in Atlanta. The desk clerk handed me a piece of paper to sign. It detailed the type of room, room rate, and my anticipated date of departure. The room rate, as agreed upon when I made the reservation, was $125 per night. I signed the paper.

At check-out, I was presented with a bill for $175 per night. When I pointed out the discrepancy to the desk clerk, I was told, "Sorry, sir, $175 is our standard room rate."

"But," I said, "$125 was the rate quoted to me over the phone."

"That's not possible," said the clerk.

How could I verify what someone had said to me over

the phone a month earlier? Aha! Fortunately, I had saved my copy of that little slip of paper they handed me at check-in.

"Here is my receipt," I told the clerk.

"Let me get the manager," he said.

"The information on this piece of paper is incorrect," the manager told me. "You'll have to pay $175 per night."

This is a classic escalation. You shake hands on a price, only to be informed later that the price was in error, a mistake was made. Your new price is higher, and now that you have already received the service, you have to pay. Another example of escalation is when you agree with a vendor on an installation or completion date, and then you are told that the date must be extended.

The escalation tactic raises ethical questions. When a vendor tells you that his price was calculated incorrectly, is he telling you the truth, or is it a ruse to get you to pay more after the fact? You have a right to demand that the vendor honor the price that was agreed upon. However, it is possible that an honest mistake was made and the vendor is entitled to some consideration—but he must prove that it was not premeditated. The burden of proof is his.

The flip side of the escalation is when the buyer tries to get away with paying *less* than the agreed-upon price. For example, you sell a used car to a buyer at an agreed-upon price of $5,000. The next day she comes to pick up the car and hands you a check for $4,500.

"We agreed on $5,000," you tell the buyer.

"But this is all I have in my bank account."

What can you do? The car has been for sale for two months, and you're glad to finally be rid of it. Plus you've already given away the floor space and even figured out how you're going to spend the money. Chances are you'll accept the $4,500. But how do you prevent this from happening? Here are a few ideas:

- Tell the buyer that you'll hold her $4,500 as a down payment. She can pay the rest next month.
- Threaten to remove the radio and CD player—or the tires.
- Tell her that the deal is off and walk away. She may suddenly discover the missing $500.

Here is how I handled the situation with the hotel in Atlanta:

"Your hotel quoted me a rate of $125 per night," I insisted to the hotel manager. "This paper confirms it. I agreed to stay here at this rate. It's too bad if you made a mistake, but that is your problem, not mine."

They accepted my payment of $125 per night.

7. *Straw Demand*

You've selected the model and color of car you want to buy. The dealer has the exact model you want—in silver—but you tell him that you really want it in blue.

"We only have it in silver," the dealer tells you. "If you take the silver car, we'll knock another $500 off the price."

Congratulations! You've just succeeded in using the straw demand, also known as the *red herring* or *decoy*. A straw demand is one that you really don't care about or expect to receive. It exists only so that you can offer to drop it in return for other concessions—ones that you really want. In the example above, the straw demand was "I want it in blue." You agreed to drop it in return for a $500 price concession.

Another way to use the straw demand is to present a laundry list of demands that you don't expect to receive. The other side may offer to drop some of its demands if you get rid of some of yours.

You can protect yourself against this tactic by understanding the difference between the other side's position and their needs. If you can figure out what is really important to them, you will be able to distinguish a real demand from straw. In that case, you still need to take the time to go over their list one by one and explain why you will not agree to certain demands.

8. The Ultimatum

We've all heard someone say, "This is not negotiable" or, "This is my final offer. Take it or leave it." This tactic is called the ultimatum. You should use an ultimatum if:

- You are adamant about your position and you want to make a strong statement that demonstrates your resolve.
- You want the other party to feel that it has pushed you to your limit.

When someone tells me, "This is non-negotiable," I regard her ultimatum simply as the beginning of negotiations. When you are presented with an ultimatum, you still have choices:

- Challenge the ultimatum (call their bluff). They may be testing you to see if you will give in. Your willingness to walk away may cause them to retract or soften the ultimatum.

- Ignore the ultimatum. Initiate a discussion of the issues, as though you never even heard their ultimatum.

When someone says, "This is not negotiable," don't take it literally. The ultimatum is usually a tactic.

9. Good Guy/Bad Guy

Remember the police show *Starsky and Hutch*? Starsky would always lean on the suspect, and Hutch would treat the suspect like a friend. To avoid a beating at Starsky's hand, the suspect would confess to a sympathetic Hutch. Good cop/bad cop is a classic law enforcement technique.

In a negotiation in which the other person is being particularly difficult, this can be a useful tactic. The opportunity to use good guy/bad guy came my way when the company I worked for was selling its assets, including the customer base, to another firm. Our best customer was being inflexible and stubborn, and our top negotiators were unable to pry any concessions from him. In fact, he insulted everyone we sent to meet with him. They would return to our offices fuming and in tears. I decided to insert myself as the bad guy. At our first meeting, this man went out of his way to offend me. I responded in kind.

"The CEO of your company must be senile to place so much responsibility with a jackass like you," I told him.

No one had ever given him a dose of his own medicine. He was flabbergasted. He called my CEO and told him, "Don't ever send that rude SOB Brodow over here again!" Exactly what I was hoping for. When my replacement, the good guy, arrived at the customer's office, he was treated with unusual respect. The nasty customer was so relieved to be rid of the bad guy—me—that he softened his behavior.

This worked because the customer never realized what we were doing. If you ever use this tactic, be careful that you don't tip your hand. If the other negotiator catches on, the game is up.

10. Surprise

You have been looking for a used BMW to give to your college-age son. After several months of searching, you finally find the car you want. It has low mileage and appears to be in excellent shape. The seller is asking $12,000. In a conversation with the seller's wife, you learn that they have not had any offers. It looks like you are in the driver's seat, so to speak. So you make a lowball offer of $8,000. Over the phone, the seller tentatively agrees. When you arrive at the seller's house, he informs you that another offer has come in for $9,000. This is the *surprise* tactic.

The purpose of the surprise is to throw you off guard. This works because you are psychologically invested in a course of action. You are committed to going through with the deal. This other offer is the last thing you were expecting, and it puts you in a weaker position. What can you do? Exercise a little patience and examine your alternatives. You can look for another car or you can call the seller's bluff and stick with your $8,000 offer. Or you can inform the other party that you need more time to evaluate the new information. The key is not to panic and immediately give in.

11. Delay/Deadline

Delay and deadline are two sides of the same coin. They are useful because of the neurotic relationship we have with time. In our culture, people are always in a hurry. Americans fall prey to these tactics when dealing with negotiators from other cultures who have a more relaxed attitude toward time.

A client of mine was assigned to negotiate a deal in Taiwan. He expected to be done in two weeks, but after three weeks the negotiation was barely under way. He took an apartment in Taipei, the capital, and it's a good thing he did. The deal took eight months to finalize. The other side was undoubtedly trying to gain more concessions by delaying the negotiation.

The delay is not the sole province of other cultures. Buyers in this country too have successfully reaped benefits from delaying negotiations. As a result, over time, sellers have developed a fitting response: the deadline.

Buyer: "We can't seem to make up our mind. Come back next week."

Seller (with a deadline): "If you don't order this week, we won't be able to deliver the product for at least three months." Or "We have a sale on this product—if you don't place the order this week, the price will go up." Or "This product is in limited supply. If you don't order now, we may run out."

Another way to cope with the delay tactic is to be patient. Remember Brodow's Law: Be willing to walk away. And if you have other options, the deadline loses its power.

12. Walking Out

I've stressed the importance of being willing to walk away from a negotiation many times in this book. It is a strategy that should not be underestimated. When you walk out of a negotiation, you are sending a powerful message that you are committed to your position and have been pushed to your limit. If the other side is under pressure to make the deal, which they probably are, chances are good that they will attempt to bring you back into the negotiation by offering concessions. Even if they do not come running after you, the tactic may still work when you return the next day.

"But how can I return after I have walked out?" I am often asked. "Doesn't my return send the message that I am giving in?"

Not if when you return, your attitude is, "Okay, I'm giving you one more chance to see things my way." Once you've walked out, they will be delighted to see you back, and be more amenable to making concessions. Practice this tactic the next time you make a retail purchase for clothing, appliances, furniture, or electronics. If they won't give you what you ask for, walk out and come back a few days later. You may be shocked at how well it works.

Sellers can use the walkout, too. If your prospective buyer refuses to pay your price, politely withdraw from the scene of battle and let him stew for a while. If the buyer really wants your product or service, he will be back.

On the other hand, you may be dealing with a savvy negotiator who is equally committed to her position. She knows that the way to deal with the walkout is to stand firm and wait for the other side to come back. If, after you have walked out a few times, the other side still refuses to budge, you can assume that you have pushed them to their limit and this is probably the best deal you are going to get.

13. The Assumptive Close

You are checking out a sofa at the furniture department of Bloomingdale's. You like the sofa, but it is rather expensive. Should you splurge or not? As you are trying to make a decision, the salesman says, "We have one of these left in stock. I can have it delivered on Saturday. Is Saturday soon enough?"

He hasn't really asked if you have decided to purchase the sofa, he has merely assumed that you have. In a way, he has done you a favor. The stress of having to make a decision has been eliminated. The salesman has made it for you.

"Uh, yes," you stutter. "Saturday? Saturday will be fine."

Okay, I know what you're thinking. This is a sales tactic, not a negotiation tactic, right? Well, not exactly. It is both. The assumptive close is a tactic that any negotiator can use. You simply assume that the other side has accepted your position and behave accordingly. When I am talking to prospective clients about doing a Negotiation Boot Camp™ seminar at their upcoming conference, I always discuss aspects of the seminar as though the deal has been done. Instead of asking, "How many hours have you allotted for a seminar?" I ask, "Are you giving me three hours or four hours?"

The buyer of a sofa is doing the same thing when she tells the salesman, "The price includes delivery, right?"

The advantage of the assumptive close is that it forces the other side to be assertive. If they don't object, you have obtained the desired result. When I was being evaluated for gum surgery, the oral surgeon did not ask me if I wanted to have the surgery. He examined me and then introduced me to his secretary.

"Alice, this is Mr. Brodow," he told her. "Schedule him for surgery next week." Then he walked away. Without missing a beat, Alice said, "What day is best for you, Mr. Brodow? Tuesday or Thursday?"

I am certain the assumptive close works on a large percentage of his patients. If I hadn't said, "Just a minute, Alice. I need to think about this," I would have ended up getting a surgery that I did not need. In negotiation, you must always be on your toes, ready to challenge the other side's assumption.

The assumptive close can be taken even one step further—to what is known as the *fait accompli*. Here's an example. Let's say you hire a contractor to repave your driveway. You agree to pay him $25 an hour, and that he will do fifteen hours of work. But pretty soon the fifteen hours are up, and he's only paved three-quarters of the driveway. He tells you he'll need five more hours, at the agreed-upon rate. What can you do? You don't want to pay another $125, but three-quarters of the job has already been completed. If he doesn't finish what he started, you'll be the laughingstock of the block and have no place to park your car. How can you handle this?

- *Nip it in the bud.* Create penalties that will deter the fait accompli. When you have a deal with contractors, insert penalties in the contract if they go over schedule or budget.
- *Scream your bloody head off.* Complaining to the

proper authority, such as the parent company or the Better Business Bureau, could reverse the fait accompli.

- *Create your own fait accompli.* Wait until the entire job is done, then send the contractor a check for the original (budgeted) amount and write "paid in full" on the back of the check. If he wants more money, let him fight for it.

14. Lowering Expectations

You finally found the house of your dreams. The sellers are asking $400,000, which is $100,000 over your budget. You are hoping they will accept a low offer of $300,000. The sellers' real estate agent informs your agent that:

- Housing prices on this street have risen 28 percent in the past year.
- *SmartMoney* magazine just named this community as one of the best places to live in the region.
- The sellers are not in a hurry to unload their house.

And so your hopes of buying your dream house at a price you can afford go up in smoke. Why? Because the sellers' real estate agent succeeded in lowering your expectations. This is a classic negotiation ploy. The antidote is to remain true to your high aspirations and be willing to walk away. You will find another dream house! Sometimes you have to let the deal go.

The good news is that you can fire back by lowering the sellers' expectations. Ask your agent to inform the sellers that:

- You are looking at two other houses.
- A comparable home on this street recently sold for $310,000.
- Your budget will not allow you to go over $300,000.

Remember, everything you say and do in a negotiation has an effect on the other negotiator's expectations.

15. Limited Authority

How many times have you heard a department store salesperson say, "I'm sorry, I don't have the authority to give you a discount"? This tactic works only when we believe them, or just don't want to take the time to argue. If someone pleads limited authority, ask, "If you don't have the authority, then who does?"

I was in Milwaukee buying a piece of luggage in a small travel store. The same item was on sale at a nearby department store.

"Can you match the department store's price?" I asked the sales clerk.

"No," she said. "I don't have the authority."

"Who does?" I asked.

"My boss."

"Can I speak to him?"

"He's not here," she said.

"Why can't *you* give me the discount?" I repeated. "Don't you want to make the sale?"

"The boss will fire me if I do," she said.

Suddenly another sales clerk, who had been listening to our conversation, jumped in.

"He's more likely to fire you if you don't make the sale," said the other clerk.

And so I received the discount, proving once again that persistence pays off.

16. Acceptance Time

In a typical negotiation, two sides try to come together from positions that can be far apart. Your position reflects your history, unique priorities, and pressures, all of which may differ greatly from your opponent's. It may take some time to find the middle ground.

This is where the concept of acceptance time comes into play. Instead of cornering your "opponent" and demanding immediate conformity to your wishes, give him a chance to get used to your ideas.

A classic example is your public utility bill. Imagine how you would feel if your power company informed you on a Friday that its electric rates were going up the following Monday.

"What! You can't do that without notice." You would be furious.

So what do they do instead? They file for a rate increase a year in advance. Six months ahead of the actual increase, you receive a letter in the mail informing you that six months from now, your rates will rise. Your reaction is muted because you are fixated on today and possibly tomorrow. Six months from now? It might as well be a decade from now. You file the letter or just throw it in the trash and get on with your life. A month before the rate increase, you receive a reminder.

"Oh yes," you remember. "That rate increase is finally going into effect."

You came to terms with it months ago without even realizing it. Why? Because the power company was smart enough to give you plenty of acceptance time.

17. Changing Negotiators

As I discussed in Week Five, changing negotiators is one way to avoid an impasse. Whenever you experience unusual difficulty in reaching agreement, it is worthwhile considering this tactic. A new negotiator brings fresh insights and is not held back by the assumptions and decisions of her predecessor.

Changing negotiators can also throw the other side off balance. If you are in sales, you probably know how upsetting it can be to find out that the buyer you have been trying to persuade for the last six months is being replaced. Once you've gotten used to his personality and negotiating style, it is tough to switch gears. Some purchasing organizations will use this tactic deliberately to prevent buyers from getting too cozy with vendors.

It will take time to get to know the new negotiator and establish a working relationship. This requires patience, a commodity that is in short supply.

18. Reverse Auction

At a classic auction, buyers bid on the seller's product. In a reverse auction, the sellers bid for the buyer's business. It works like this. You are buying a new telephone system for your company. Three vendors are bidding for the job. You arrange to have Vendor One come in at 10:00 A.M., Vendor Two at 10:30, and Vendor Three at 11:00. Each of them knows that the others are making their bids. This puts maximum pressure on them to lower their rates, relieving you of the pressure of having to offer them the most attractive deal.

I am often asked by sellers: "How can we cope with a bidding war?" A reverse auction or a bid situation does not alter the essential buying criterion: The buyer wants the best solution to its problem. A seller who is able to solve the buyer's problem better than the competition can demand a higher price. If you are a seller and are tempted to meet a competitor's lower bid, keep the following in mind:

- If you drop your price, the buyer will think that your product is worth less.
- For most buyers, price is not their main criterion—regardless of what they say and how they behave.
- The best way to cope with a reverse auction is to do your selling in advance. If you wait until the last minute, it may be too late. When you have convinced the buyer earlier on, he may weigh the entire process in your favor by writing the specification around your product (see Week Nine: Buyers and Sellers).

19. Humor

I want to share with you a personal secret that has been of great value to me over the years. I am a strong believer in the value of humor in negotiation. Humor does three things. First, it can really lighten things up and dissolve the tension.

It makes people feel more comfortable, and it shows that you don't take yourself too seriously.

Second, humor makes it easier to be tough without offending anybody. I remember a sales presentation in which we asked the buyer, "Are we in the ballpark?" He said, "Boys, you don't even have gloves!" We roared with laughter, but we got the message. He managed to score a very tough point without offending us—by making his point funny.

Third, if you want to avoid answering a question, make a joke out of it. A friend of mine was attempting to sell a complex multimillion-dollar telephone system to a large hospital when the customer asked to see a comparable system in action. My buddy took them to view a phone system his firm had installed in a nearby psychiatric hospital. One of the areas they visited was the main telephone console, which—unknown to my friend—was being operated by a patient.

"What do you think of this phone system?" the prospective customer asked the console operator.

"It stinks!" she said.

The prospective customer turned to my friend and said, "What are you going to do about that?"

"I'm never going to hire her to work for me," my friend replied.

They laughed so hard that the entire issue was forgotten. The sale was made in spite of the console operator's comment.

So remember, laugh, and the world laughs with you!

20. Telephone Tactics

Negotiating over the telephone is an art in itself. Because 90 percent of communication is nonverbal, the phone effectively cuts us off from most of the information we use to make decisions in a negotiation. You can't read my body language. You can't tell if I'm perspiring or if my facial muscles are all tensed up. But you can overcome this by following a few simple rules:

1. *Buffer your calls.*

When you answer the phone, you are entering into a conversation unprepared. But the person on the other end is prepared. He knew about the call in advance. You didn't know about it until the phone rang. Your lack of preparedness places you at a distinct disadvantage. You may give away information that should be kept under wraps or make concessions that you will regret later on. You can protect yourself by buffering your calls—building in a safeguard that allows you to postpone the negotiation until you are better prepared. Here are some ways to do this:

- Have a secretary or receptionist screen your calls. If you are not ready to negotiate, ask the screener to take a message or tell the callers that you will call them back.
- Let the call go to voice mail.
- Refuse to talk: "I'm on the other line/in a conference/ due in a meeting/about to take a shower. Can I call you back?"

2. *Follow the 70/30 Rule.*

Keeping your mouth shut is even more important over the phone than in person. Listen more than you speak. Give the other negotiator plenty of opportunities to make mistakes by shooting his big mouth off. The less you say, the fewer mistakes you will make. In case you forgot, the 70/30 Rule is: Listen 70 percent of the time, and talk 30 percent (see Week Two).

3. *Don't be in a hurry to agree.*

There is something funny about that little telephone in your hand. It makes you want to get the negotiation over with quickly. It encourages you to agree without giving due consideration to the issues at hand. Be aware of this tendency. If you are not ready to commit, or if you have any reservations whatsoever, put off a decision. This is one time when vacillating is a good idea. Tell the other person that you need to "sleep on it."

4. *Write a deal memo.*

The problem with verbal agreements is that few of us can later remember exactly who said what and to whom. "I never said that." "What do you mean, we agreed to do such-and-such?" If you make a verbal agreement over the telephone, the only way to protect yourself from misunderstandings is to write a deal memo that succinctly states the terms that were agreed upon and confirms the understanding of the parties. If you can be the author of the deal memo, so much the better, as the version of what took place will be your version. Fax or e-mail your deal memo to the other party. Get them to acknowledge that they received it and sign off on it. You have just prevented them from denying their agreement later on.

WEEK NINE

Buyers and Sellers

Everything is worth what its purchaser will pay for it.

—PUBLIUS SYRUS

Negotiation has always been all about buying and selling. Even when we are not buying and selling in the literal sense, we still are buying and selling ideas. In Week Nine we will examine the negotiation process from these two perspectives. Let's begin with the buyer.

NEGOTIATION FOR BUYERS

Ten Tips for Convincing the Seller to Take Less

The classic negotiating challenge for buyers is to obtain better pricing and terms from vendors. Here are ten tips to help you do this.

Tip Number One: Prices are not chiseled in stone.

Whenever you see a price tag, imagine that it says, "This is what we'd like to get." Here is where negotiation consciousness comes into play. If you don't ask for concessions, you may be leaving money on the table. Buyers must consider how badly the seller needs to sell. The seller may have little confidence in his own pricing structure and may be looking for an excuse to give the buyer a discount.

Tip Number Two: Use the power of competition.

Sellers will often jump at the opportunity to match or beat a competitor's price. "You gotta do better." The *squeeze* works when they know you have the option of buying from somebody else. Make it clear that you would prefer to buy from them, but you cannot justify the purchase when another vendor is offering substantially better terms.

Tip Number Three: Present a Sob Story.

Point out the limits of your budget. Tell the seller you love the product, but you simply can't afford it. Many salespeople will support you by telling their superiors that the sale will be lost if a discount is not forthcoming, especially on pricier items.

Tip Number Four: Lower the seller's expectations.

Everything you say and do in a negotiation affects the seller's expectations. If you open with an extreme position—offer less than you are actually willing to pay—the seller will often be on the run. Another way to lower his expectations is to suggest that you really don't need the product, and make it clear that you are prepared to walk out.

Tip Number Five: Force a delay.

One of the tactics that drives salespeople crazy is the *delay*. The poor seller is trying to make his quota, but the buyer keeps putting off the purchase. If the seller is in a hurry to make the sale, he's likely to eventually give the patient buyer a discount.

Tip Number Six: Nibble.

If you can't get what you want up front, try to tack it on after the deal is made. The seller may be forced to maintain his pricing structure, but he may be able to give you other concessions that can add up in value. Even if you've already agreed on a price, you can nibble for additional products or services, for faster delivery and service, or for a myriad of other possibilities that are limited only by your imagination.

Tip Number Seven: Split the order.

If the seller won't budge on price, consider breaking the order into its component parts and obtaining some of those parts from somebody else. Buy from this seller only what you cannot obtain elsewhere. Large manufacturers such as General Motors do this with most of their purchasing; each component of a GM automobile is sourced separately to ensure getting the best deals. On a smaller scale, when you are buying a home entertainment center, don't feel obligated to purchase everything from one store. Find the best vendor for each element—the television monitor, audio speakers, receiver, cable, and so on.

Tip Number Eight: Find the exception.

Often, the seller will not give you a better deal because he fears he will then be obligated to do the same for other buyers. Get around this obstacle by making your purchase an exception. For example: Instead of buying one of the dozen models in the stockroom, see if you can get a deal on last season's model, a product with slight defects, or a floor sample. The seller will likely be eager to get rid of these, and if another buyer asks the seller for the same deal you received, the seller can reply, "I'm so sorry, that was our only floor sample."

Tip Number Nine: Force the seller to commit time and effort.

The seller will be more inclined to give you a discount after she has invested substantial time and effort to getting your business. For example, if you take up several hours of a car salesperson's time, she will be more motivated to give you a special deal so the time she spent with you will not have been wasted. Getting other people in her company involved in its attempt to sell you increases the commitment, too.

Tip Number Ten: Buy in volume.

Many firms waste millions each year because they are not capitalizing on the power of buying in bulk. Few sellers will refuse to lower the price if you buy in large volume. Find ways to pool your buying so you can obtain a bulk discount.

Going against a Price Increase

What do you do when a seller tries to raise the price above a listing or sticker price? Here are some tips:

Tip Number One: Negotiate for the most favored customer price.

Get the best deal offered by the sellers. If they have offered someone else a better deal, demand that they offer it to you as well.

Tip Number Two: Limit the increase.

If an increase is unavoidable, ask the seller to limit or reduce the amount.

Tip Number Three: Tie the escalation to a standard.

Invoke a "not to exceed" limit. The standard can be the Consumer Price Index, or another mutually acceptable criterion.

Eight Tips for Dealing with a Sole Source

The most frustrating situation for a buyer is to be confronted with a *sole source,* in other words, when only one seller offers the product or service. Where can you find negotiating power when dealing with a sole source? Here are a few ideas:

Tip Number One: Buy another type of product.

Buy a Dell or HP computer instead of an Apple, or a Corolla instead of a Mini Cooper, or an LCD TV screen instead of plasma. Just because the seller is the only one who makes a particular product doesn't mean that you can't find a competing one.

Tip Number Two: Buy it used.

If the seller won't give in, consider buying a "previously owned" model, or a discontinued model. Many Internet sites (such as eBay) offer used models no longer found in stores.

Tip Number Three: Rent it.

If you can't buy at a reasonable price, consider renting it where applicable. Or go through a distributor who may offer a better deal than the manufacturer.

Tip Number Four: Bundle products.

Create leverage by including other items in your purchase, or increase the size of the order.

Tip Number Five: Threaten to do without it.

If you are a major user of the product, your threat will be taken seriously.

Tip Number Six: Create the impression that competition exists.

If you give the seller the impression that you have found another source, he may soften his position in order to hang on to your business. If the seller doesn't know his product is the only one that meets your specs, don't tell him.

Tip Number Seven: Allude to the possibility of future competition.

Convince him that the long-term interest of having you as a customer outweighs the short-term gain of not making any concessions. If he treats you badly, let him know that you will jump ship when competitive products appear.

Tip Number Eight: Buy the seller out.

If you have the means, consider making a strategic acquisition.

Warning to the Aggressive Buyer

In the early 1990s, General Motors, then America's largest automobile company, decided to play hardball with its suppliers. Under orders from a new head of procurement, José Ignacio Lopez de Arriortua, GM notified all of its suppliers that they were expected to reduce their prices by at least 10 percent. Lopez gave no consideration to the cost of producing the parts, or to whether or not suppliers would lose money by dropping their prices. They were given only two choices: They could lower their prices, or GM would drop them.

From 1992–93, Lopez's hardball maneuver reportedly saved GM approximately $4 billion in expenses. Did he do GM a favor? In spite of the savings, Lopez is widely criticized for damaging GM's long-term supplier relationships and, as a result, its future competitiveness. While some suppliers caved in to Lopez's strong-arm tactics, many started giving their cutting-edge technology to Ford and Chrysler rather than to GM, according to Ed Rigsbee in *The Art of Partnering*. Some GM suppliers were so turned off by Lopez's way of doing business that they took their technology overseas or to other industries. The result? GM opened the 1995 Detroit Auto Show without any new models to offer the public.

In other words, Lopez's strategy backfired. GM enjoyed a short-term benefit from its cutthroat purchasing strategy, but paid a heavy price in the long run.

Moral of the story: Don't push your vendors too far. If you push them off the cliff, they just might take you with them.

NEGOTIATION FOR SELLERS

The Pitfalls of Price Negotiating

One of my clients makes and sells software that helps businesses run their complex computer systems. This client was contacted by a large manufacturer who wanted to purchase $2 million worth of software—a sizable deal for my client. The buyer claimed that one of my client's competitors offered a comparable software system for half the price. If my client wanted the deal, the buyer said, he would have to match the competitor's offer.

In reality, although the competitor's company did make the same *type* of software, its product was not as sophisticated as my client's, and would not solve the main problem in the buyer's current computer setup, which was the very reason for the purchase. However, the buyer attempted to hide this fact from my client.

In order to close the sale, my client had to concede major discounts that rendered the deal unprofitable. Had he been aware of the buyer's true situation and recognized his own product's superiority over the competition's, he could have closed the deal at a much higher price—and enjoyed a profit.

This is not an example of poor business sense. My client was extremely knowledgeable about his product and the marketplace. However, this knowledge became a drawback because it prevented him from probing further. He thought he knew all he needed to know, and in his cockiness simply forgot to fulfill his obligation as detective—to uncover the buyer's real need. Instead of listening to the buyer, he rashly offered price discounts and missed out on what could have been a profitable transaction.

The lesson: Don't jump to lower your prices until you have done all your homework.

Nine Tips for Convincing the Buyer to Pay More

Every salesperson eventually must confront the following situation:

- You want the deal badly.
- You need the business.
- You've been suspecting that the price of your product or service is too high to begin with.

So what do you do? You lower your price rather than negotiate. Many salespeople are afraid to stand by their price structure because of a single mistaken assumption: "If I refuse to negotiate my price, I'll lose all my customers." The reality is just the opposite. If you aren't prepared to defend your price, your customers will lose respect for you.

Here are nine tips that will help you negotiate the price you deserve:

Tip Number One: You are entitled to reasonable compensation.

Just as your doctor, your accountant, and your plumber are entitled to a reasonable compensation for their services, so are you. What is reasonable? Whatever you can convince your buyer that your product or service is worth. The operative principle here is value. No buyer will begrudge you a price that is reasonable relative to the perceived value of the product/service.

Tip Number Two: Don't sell yourself short!

Do you believe that what you are selling is worth the price? If the answer is yes, and I certainly hope it is, then you should expect to receive worthy compensation. If you lack confidence about your product or service, buyers will sense your doubts. Have you noticed the range of prices for similar products and services? It fascinates me when some salespeople are able to bring in the order at a premium price while others can't seem to get by without discounting. What accounts for this? One salesperson gets up in the morning and says, "My product is great and my customers are happy to pay my price!" Another salesperson gets up and says, "My product is okay, but the buyer will never pay me such-and-such!" Don't sell yourself short.

Tip Number Three: Don't apologize!

Once you have established the value of your product or service, present your price with confidence. Never apologize for it. If you believe your price is correct, just assume that your customers will agree.

Tip Number Four: Always be willing to walk away!

You must be prepared to say "Next!" or your customers will sense your uncertainty. The willingness to walk away from a sale comes from having other potential sales in the lineup. When you know that your sales career doesn't hinge on this one deal, you can exude confidence. And buyers will bow to it.

Tip Number Five: How to justify your price.

Once you have decided on your price, you must provide reasonable justification so your buyer will say, "Okay, that makes sense. I can accept that." Here is how:

1. Give your price legitimacy: "My price is reasonable for the marketplace. This is the going price for this product or service." If your buyers are doing their homework, they will know you are telling the truth.
2. Focus on the value of your product/service, not on the price. Buyers will pay for value. Highlight features and benefits.
3. Explain that you'd like to help them out, but you can't because you can't lower your price for one customer without lowering your price for everybody. Claim limited authority.

Tip Number Six: When to negotiate your price.

Obviously there are exceptions. You want to leave yourself the option of negotiating a lower price if it is in your best interest to do so. The operative principle here is called "saving face." In other words, you will lower your price only if you can save face, that is, maintain the integrity of your basic pricing structure. So you tell your customer, "I accept a lower price only under the following circumstances . . ."

What are those circumstances? You might consider offering a discount if the customer will buy more than one, or if the merchandise is flawed. I once gave a keynote speech at a reduced fee for a client who had already booked six two-day seminars (a volume discount). My face-saver: the multiple bookings. (As a result of the interest generated by the keynote, the client booked another six seminars.)

Tip Number Seven: How to negotiate your price.

If one of these exceptions applies, and it makes sense for you to negotiate your price, the following basic rules should be part of your arsenal.

1. *Focus on value.* Take the focus off the price by reselling the total package: value-added, features and benefits. Concentrate on what it's worth.

2. *Don't be afraid to repeat yourself.* The buyer may not hear every point the first time around. Persistence pays off.

3. *Allow the buyer to let off steam.* The buyer's objections are healthy. He is trying to convince himself that it is okay to buy from you. Remember from Week Two that it's never a good idea to interrupt a buyer who is contemplating a purchase. Don't interfere with his process by cutting him off.

4. *Flinch.* The buyer may be testing you by challenging your price. If you flinch—"You want to pay how much? Are you serious?"—the buyer may back off. Just be careful you do not offend the buyer.

5. *Make minor concessions.* Instead of lowering your price, offer something extra that doesn't cost you a lot (like a warranty, or free delivery) but which the buyer will appreciate.

6. *Make use of the buyer's fears.* Chances are the buyer is afraid of making a wrong decision. Why not let her believe disaster will strike if she chooses to go with the competitor's inferior product?

7. *Tie a string.* If you feel you must offer a discount, make it contingent upon receiving a concession from the buyer.

Tip Number Eight: Don't be too quick to make concessions.

If you appear too anxious to negotiate your price or terms downward, the buyer will perceive this as an admission that your product is worth less than your asking price. One of my favorite price negotiations was with a client who received a proposal from a competitor who wanted the job so badly that he offered to do a negotiation seminar for nothing (just to break into the account). My client tried to convince me that I should lower my fee, but I politely refused. In the end, the client booked me because it viewed my competitor's presentation as worth the price—namely zero. My seminar was perceived as being more valuable due to my confidence in my fee.

Tip Number Nine: Qualify your prospective buyers.

There are occasions in which negotiating with a customer may be a waste of your time. If you think a buyer may be out of your price range (either below it or above it), ask at the outset: "What kind of budget do you have?" or "What range are we looking at here?" You may not be on the same playing field. If this is the case, you may want to push a more or a less expensive item. Or you may want to fit the customer into an exception category—provided that you can save face.

Whatever you do, remember that your objective is to create a satisfied customer.

NEGOTIATING A PRICE INCREASE

Negotiating a price increase can be tricky. Here are some strategies you should use:

1. *Raise prices after a victory.* If your product has just won an award or saved your customer a significant amount of time or money, it's a good time to try to raise the price.

2. *Give the buyer advance notice.* Dropping a price increase in the buyer's lap with no warning is a slap in the face. Give your customer some time to get used to the idea. (Remember what we learned about Acceptance Time in Week Eight.)

3. *Legitimize the increase.* If you can provide good reasons, it will be easier for the buyer to accept your increase. "We are forced to raise prices because the cost of raw materials has gone up."

4. *Allow the buyer to vent his displeasure.* The buyer is going to be upset with any price increase. You must give him a chance to express his anger, or else he will bear a grudge. If you can, be there in person and listen.

5. *Include something extra or new.* When the price of a tube of toothpaste goes up, notice how the package will suddenly boast some new feature—"New, improved formula." Create the perception that the customer is receiving extra value for his extra money.

6. *Compromise the increase.* Offer to phase in the increase in installments. Five percent now, five percent in six months.

7. *Offer less for the same price.* This is a common practice in consumer goods—rather than raise the price, the quantity or volume is reduced to save costs. Repair shops sometimes keep their basic costs at the same level, but start charging for auxiliary services that used to be

free (such as putting air in our car tires, or calling direc-
tory assistance).   .

The major obstacle that prevents salespeople from asking for the price they want is the fear of rejection. The best
way to overcome this fear is to school yourself in assertive
negotiation techniques. If you are assertive, your belief in
yourself and your product or service will be your best
weapon. Your confidence will be rewarded.

SELLING VIA FORMAL BIDDING

A bid situation presents a special challenge to the salesperson. When bids are involved, the seller is deprived of having
direct access to the buyer. Many sellers succumb to this
pressure by lowering their expectations and their prices.
Here are some suggestions for coping with the bidding
process:

1. *The real selling must occur before the bidding process
   begins*. The bidding begins when the buyer issues an
   RFP (request for proposal) to a group of approved vendors. The seller should begin selling before the RFP goes
   out. A smart salesperson will convince the client to
   write its RFP around the seller's product/service. This is
   where organizational selling comes in. If the seller has
   infiltrated all levels of the buyer's organization, the
   buyer will be inclined to write specifications that favor
   the seller's product.
2. *Submit multiple bids.*
       a. Submit one bid based upon the buyer's specifica-
          tions.

b. Submit a second bid based upon what could be done if the buyer's specs were more flexible.

3. *Try to be the last bidder.* The last bidder always has an advantage because the buyer learns something new with each bid. If you are last, you can benefit from the buyer's enhanced awareness.

4. *Negotiate with your pricing people.* You can still negotiate with the buyer—on changes and additions—after you get the deal.

5. *Remain available to the buyer.* Explain your bid and answer questions as the need arises.

WEEK TEN

Workplace Negotiations between
Managers and Employees

I don't believe in just ordering people to do things. You have to sort
of grab an oar and row with them.

—HAROLD GENEEN

The process of managing people is a form of negotiation; it is an agreement about how a job ought to be performed. The manager wants his subordinate to do the job in a way that corresponds to his vision. The subordinate often wants to do things his own way. What does it take to be a good manager? I have been both a manager and a subordinate, and I can tell you from experience that good managers are hard to find. Here are some of the adjectives I often hear people use to describe their managers:

Rigid, grandiose, paranoid, controlling, bullying, dictatorial, antisocial.

With the wonderful business schools we have in this country, why are there so many bad managers running around? Because many are lacking in the critical area of interpersonal negotiation. Many have not been trained in the negotiating techniques that are necessary to motivate people. As a result, many are incapable of motivating a thirsty man to get a drink of water.

THE BONOBO SYSTEM OF MANAGEMENT

Let's compare the two main types of negotiation with the task of managing people. The managing equivalent of adversarial negotiation is the hardball style epitomized by Donald Trump on his TV show, *The Apprentice*. Employees are told, if they don't measure up, "YOU'RE FIRED!" During my corporate days, I had one boss who would have loved *The Apprentice*. I was one of eight experienced sales representatives transferred to his department from another division. On our first day in the new department we were ushered into his office, shook hands, and sat down. I will never forget the first thing he said to us.

"I fired 125 people last year and I'm proud of it!"

Not "Good morning," or "Welcome to my department."

Imagine the effect his statement had on us, a group of men with families to support. Were we motivated? Inspired? I know that I wasn't. I was disgusted. This approach to managing people—management by fear—has long been the norm in the corporate world, and I believe it accounts for much of the dissatisfaction in the workplace. Studies have shown that the number one reason for stress on the job is the boss. I believe that if the goal of management is to get employees to do what they want, this style of management by fear is counterproductive.

I prefer what I call the *Bonobo System of Management*. Bonobo managers apply the Three Rules for Win-Win Negotiating to create a work atmosphere that preserves the dignity of the employees.

1. *Change your behavior from adversarial to cooperative.*

Treat each employee as an individual. The bonobo manager finds a way to utilize each person's unique attributes to foster cooperation in service of the company. He does not try to intimidate his employees, but rather encourages them to apply their strengths in areas where they can make the optimum contribution.

When I worked as a sales rep for IBM in the seventies, I once alerted my manager to a threat from a competitor who was going after our largest customer. Unfortunately for him, my manager didn't see me as an individual who could make a genuine contribution to the company.

"You are just a junior marketing representative," he told me. "You don't have the necessary experience to be able to analyze our overall account strategy. You couldn't possibly be right about this situation."

He was wrong. My prediction turned out to be dead-on accurate. But by the time my manager saw it coming, it was too late. It taught me a lesson. When I became a sales manager at Litton Industries, I tried to view each of my reps as a partner rather than a subordinate, each with a set of unique skills. Our product line consisted mainly of complex systems that required a certain knowledge on the part of the sales reps. When it came to my attention that one of my reps didn't have a sophisticated understanding of our big, complex systems, instead of firing or demoting him, I asked him to concentrate on smaller systems. It worked. He broke the company record for selling small systems. Had I taken the Trumplike approach and punished him for his poor performance with the complex systems, I would have lost a valuable member of our sales team.

2. *Develop trust by listening.*

A client with a network of dental offices set up a series of procedures for his employees to follow when dealing with patients (for example, a patient who has been in the waiting room for fifteen minutes must be moved into a treatment room). But his employees refused to follow the rules. My client took an adversarial position, treating the employees with disrespect. "I'm the boss, do as I say" was his attitude. He scolded, threatened, and even fired one person as an example to the others. Nothing worked until we convinced the client to show respect for his employees by listening. So he set up a meeting in which the staff could air their grievances and make suggestions on how to improve the existing rules. My client finally heard what they had to say, and together they created a new set of office procedures they were happy to follow and that ended up being much more effective. Employees are more productive when their manager takes the time to listen.

3. *Explore options for mutual satisfaction.*

One leading cause of workplace stress is confusion over expectations. When the employee has clear guidelines for his job objectives, this confusion disappears. Managing employee expectations, then, is a function of stating clear objectives. The best manager I ever had would first describe the task and then give me options for how to accomplish it in my own way. It was the most productive period in my corporate career. The bonobo manager does not say, "Do it this way because I say so." He describes the objective, telling his subordinates what to do but *not how to do it.* If an employee's skill set is in sync with her position, and she understands her objectives, she will get the job done. The manager's function is to provide clear options that lead to the desired result.

Here are more tips for becoming a bonobo-style manager:

1. *Involve subordinates in decision making.*

The bonobo manager makes his subordinates feel that their decisions are their own. He listens to what they have to say and he asks their opinion. Because they are involved in the process, they have a stake in the outcome. They can later see where they contributed to the end product, and they enjoy a sense of completion. Workers who feel that they are an integral part of an operation are far more productive than those who do not. In the cooperative system of management, employees who are able to see the fruits of their labor and their ideas derive a strong sense of satisfaction from their jobs.

2. *Give constructive criticism.*

People who manage by fear are often abusive in their application of criticism. In adversarial management, criticism is a tool for bullying. The cooperative manager, however, uses *constructive criticism:* criticism that encourages you to correct the mistake without insulting or offending. Sometimes criticism is called for, but if it is delivered in an objective, affirming, and kind way, it will make the employee want to do better in the future, not feel shame about his mistakes.

3. *Use meetings as a tool for sharing ideas.*

Meetings seem to be a necessary tool in the business world. Unfortunately, they often serve as venues for managers to assert their authority rather than as tools for communication. In a bonobo corporation, the two main functions of meetings are (a) for the manager to share information with the group, and (b) for the group to share ideas, thoughts, and suggestions among themselves and with management. For the manager, the meeting is an opportunity to listen and learn. For the group, it is a chance to participate and be heard.

NEGOTIATING WITH SUPERIORS: TAKING ON THE BULLY

I have observed a tendency for employees to allow themselves to be intimidated by abusive superiors. In my view this is counterproductive. Showing intimidation gives the impression that you lack confidence, which implies that you don't know what you are doing. So how can an employee negotiate with a boss who is abusive?

A corporate client hired me to train its support staff in how to deal with abusive behavior by senior partners. One of the responsibilities of the support staff was to arrange for private cars to transport partners to and from home and office. If a problem arose with the car service, the partner would typically verbally abuse the support person who had arranged the ride. The partners were highly paid professionals who had forgotten that the support staff were also human beings. And the support personnel believed that they had to accept this abuse or lose their jobs. The support employees needed to build their self-esteem. When they felt better about themselves, and realized that they were entitled to common courtesy even from a senior partner, they were better able to serve the highly strung partners without creating more hostility. We taught them two techniques:

1. *Confront the abusive behavior in a constructive, amicable way.*

Abusive behavior must be confronted or it will continue. But you have a choice to make. Like any other negotiation, an abusive boss can be confronted in an adversarial way or in a cooperative way. Adversarial behavior is characterized by hostility, sarcasm, and destructive criticism; the adversarial way to confront a boss who behaves like a bully is to yell back at him and treat him the way he has treated you. This will only make matters worse. On the other hand, cooperative behavior is constructive and focuses on achieving a mutually satisfactory result. The cooperative way to deal with the abusive boss is to explain—in emotionally neutral terms—how his behavior is having a negative effect on your job performance.

Remember the "I" statement from Week One? Instead of saying, "You are an abusive so-and-so and I hate your guts," take responsibility for your feelings and instead say, "When I am treated in an overbearing way, I get the feeling that you regard me as an ineffective employee. It undermines my enthusiasm for the job. I would be grateful if, in the future, you would give me constructive criticism—including a pat on the back when you think I have earned one." You have not attacked your boss. Instead of behaving like a victim, you have acted assertively, letting him know what you need from him.

2. *The Confidence Mystique.*

People bow to confidence. As we discussed in Week Three, your boss will have more respect for you if you give off the signal that you are in charge, that you know what you're doing.

I have spoken to many meeting planner groups, people responsible for making the necessary arrangements for company meetings. These groups consist primarily of women, most of whom have been promoted from secretarial or support positions. As a result, many lack the confidence to stand up to their male superiors. They are often given instructions from a senior manager to hold the meeting at an expensive venue. This creates a conflict between the planner's desire to stay within budget restrictions and her desire to please the manager. If she succumbs to the manager's intimidation, she will go over budget; if not, she risks angering or disappointing the manager. It's a lose-lose situation.

The meeting planner's sole option, I believe, is to confront the senior manager with confidence and explain the realities of the budget and the available options. After all, she is the expert on meetings, not him. If she projects this, he will be likely to curb the abuse and accept her advice.

WEEK ELEVEN

Negotiating in the Flat World

Everyone is a prisoner of his own experiences.

—EDWARD R. MURROW

In the summer of 1962 the Soviet Union secretly installed offensive nuclear weapons in Cuba. Up to that point the United States had been the only nation with a long-range nuclear capability—we could hit the Russians but they could not hit us. The new Cuban launchpad gave the Soviets a potential nuclear shot at U.S. soil for the very first time. When, on October 15, U.S. spy planes discovered the existence of the missiles in Cuba, the American government was both outraged and terrified. On October 22, President John F. Kennedy demanded that the USSR remove all its missiles from the island. Any nuclear missile fired from Cuba, Kennedy warned, would be regarded as an attack on the United States.

On October 25, Kennedy raised U.S. military readiness almost to an all-out alert. The men with the doomsday buttons were standing by. Premier Khrushchev of the USSR offered to remove the missiles *if and only if* the United States would promise not to invade Cuba. A clear opportunity for a win-win agreement. We would be rid of the missiles and the Soviets would save face. But Kennedy refused.

On October 27 an American U-2 spy plane accidentally wandered into Soviet airspace, nearly causing a nuclear exchange. At the same time Khrushchev upped the ante, demanding that Kennedy remove American missiles in Turkey. Kennedy did not want to comply because he was afraid of losing face politically.

Meanwhile, on Fidel Castro's orders, the Cubans shot down an American U-2 aircraft. The U.S. military, headed by hawkish Gen. Curtis LeMay, urged the president to attack Cuba. "I thought I might never live to see another Saturday night," reminisced former secretary of defense Robert McNamara. The world stood at the brink of nuclear war.

On October 28 the stalemate ended when the United States agreed to Khruschev's original demand and issued a guarantee that we would not invade Cuba. Khrushchev, summarily, agreed to remove his missiles. Nuclear winter was avoided by a hair.

The Cuban Missile Crisis could have been avoided altogether if the two parties had used win-win negotiation techniques. Each side had fed on the other's hostility, and neither side was listening. No one had attempted to create an atmosphere of trust, nor did they explore options for mutual satisfaction. But another factor was at play in this epic near-disaster. The two sides had come to the table from two highly divergent cultural perspectives.

The autocratic Russians were accustomed to an autocratic style of leadership. The Americans viewed the conflict through the eyes of a democracy. The Cold War was a conflict between two systems that were polar opposites, politically and economically. Neither side took time to understand the cultural differences that separated them.

The same problem shows up today in international business. American companies don't always understand the customs when negotiating in foreign markets. And businesspeople from other cultures, too, often have trouble connecting with Western negotiators.

But we have no choice other than to learn to overcome these cultural barriers. In our flattening world, like it or not, we are increasingly going to be negotiating with people who differ from us. Can it really be that difficult? The first thing you must do before going to a foreign country to negotiate is to research its customs. The library is full of books describing the business and social etiquette in China or Brazil or wherever you happen to be heading, and the Internet is flooded with sites and blogs that do the same. Or simply ask around—chances are one of your friends or colleagues has had experience doing business with people from other cultures and may have some valuable advice to share. Each culture, of course, is different, but certain themes appear to be constant throughout the world. Here are what I believe to be the four essential elements to take into account when negotiating with people from other cultures.

1. SHOW RESPECT

Since World War II, the United States has enjoyed a privileged status in the world. English has become the default language of business and culture. We sometimes forget that the planet is full of varied cultures with rich histories, and that the people who inhabit them are proud of their heritage and resent the "ugly American" who behaves as though his culture has no equal.

I have traveled extensively in France and Japan, two countries that have ancient and proud cultures. Both the French and the Japanese are often said to be somewhat aloof and unwilling to accept foreigners. In my experience, however, the French people have been consistently polite and friendly because I always make the attempt, albeit clumsy at times, to reach out to them. When I try to speak my imperfect Berlitz French before I revert to English, their faces light up in appreciation of my effort. They recognize my attempt to speak to them in French as a sign of my respect for their culture, and return my respect accordingly. The same is true for the Japanese. Upon demonstrating an appreciation for their culture, I have been hospitably invited to stay in the homes of Japanese people who were little more than strangers.

So if you want to succeed with foreign negotiators, make sure you show the respect that their culture deserves.

2. EXERCISE PATIENCE

Westerners have a warped sense of time. We are always in a hurry, always neglecting to savor the beauty of the moment. Spending time in other countries has convinced me that most cultures have much better attitudes when it comes to time. While we always want to get everything over with as quickly as possible, the rest of the world is on a different time clock. Whether you are in Asia, Latin America, Africa, or the Middle East, patience is the hallmark of negotiation.

They want to get to know you. They want to feel comfortable about making a deal with you. And they are accustomed to taking their time going about it.

Americans often shoot themselves in the foot by expecting to do business abroad as quickly as they are accustomed to doing business at home. My clients often tell me about how they made a business trip to Japan with the assumption that they would conclude negotiations in a few days. Typically, the story goes like this: "Instead of getting down to business, my Japanese hosts wined and dined me, took me around to visit the sights, and only after a week or more did they show any willingness to begin negotiations. I spent three weeks doing what should have taken three days!" The Japanese understand our impatience and use it as a tactic in gaining concessions.

When you leave American shores, think of Einstein's Theory of Relativity. Time expands . . . Slow down.

3. NURTURE PERSONAL RELATIONSHIPS

Our way of doing business is rather impersonal. We rarely get to know the people we negotiate with outside of the negotiation, except perhaps for the occasional drink or game of golf. Not so in many foreign cultures. The other negotiators need to trust you, and in order to do so they expect to get to know all about who you are.

In Western countries we depend upon contracts and legal documents to protect us if something goes wrong with an agreement. In the United States we have a population of approximately 300 million people, and 700,000 of them are lawyers. In Japan there are 150 million people, and only 10,000 lawyers in the whole country. This is because in

Japan, agreements are protected by personal, not contractual, relationships. If one party to a deal has difficulty meeting its end of the agreement, the other party is expected to work something out without resorting to attorneys.

If you intend to do business abroad, expect to develop close personal relationships, and be prepared to invest the time it takes to do so.

4. NEGOTIATE OFF THE RECORD

It often seems that in America, everything we do and say is reduced to paper. We conduct our negotiations in formal sessions first, then we write the terms down on a piece of paper, sign our names, and suddenly it's a legally binding agreement that might as well be set in stone.

When personal relationships take precedence over contracts, it makes sense that much of the negotiating would be informal. People in many other cultures prefer the intimacy that comes with negotiating in social situations to the formality of an office or boardroom. It can be disconcerting for the American newly arrived in Japan, for example, to discover that his negotiating counterparts want to take him sightseeing. "I came here to make a deal, not to drink sake!" But informal settings can be productive because they foster cooperation and trust. Don't resist the less harried customs of your overseas business partners. "When in Rome," as the old saying goes, "do as the Romans do."

WEEK TWELVE

Ten Things People Don't Realize
They Can Negotiate For

I would prefer not to.

—HERMAN MELVILLE, *BARTLEBY THE SCRIVENER*

I will never forget one Negotiation Boot Camp™ seminar I once gave, during which a participant refused to believe my assertion that retail items can be negotiated.

"When I walk into a store, I am implicitly agreeing to accept their prices," she argued. "That sort of thing *just isn't done!*"

Week Twelve of *Negotiation Boot Camp* focuses on negotiating everyday things that one might not realize are even negotable. Many people are reluctant to exercise their bargaining power. In my seminars, when I discuss ways to expand one's paycheck by negotiating, participants will often say, "But I can't do that. Can I?" Even sophisticated business executives are bearish when it comes to what is and is not negotiable. Here are a few things you may not have thought were negotiable, but in fact are.

1. SALARY: GIVE YOURSELF A RAISE

Many of us dislike negotiating because we are afraid of being shot down, especially when we believe that we are in a weak position. Salary negotiations provide a classic example. Has the fear of losing the job or angering your boss kept you from trying to negotiate a salary you deserve? This fear is fostered by the "management by intimidation" I discussed in Week Ten. The truth is, if your boss values your services, he won't fire you for being assertive—he may even respect you more for it.

Here is my twelve-step process for negotiating your salary without fear.

1. Study the situation.

Before negotiating your salary or asking for a raise, do some research. What are the organization's norms on salaries? Is there an established range for your position? What are other people in comparable positions inside the organization being paid? What do other companies pay for this position? How important are you to the organization? If others are being paid more, and you are a key employee, be assertive (see number 5). If the policy is not to pay what you want, and you're replaceable—be prepared to walk (see Number 12).

2. Know what you want.

This may sound obvious, but in reality, many people negotiate for a salary without having a clear idea of what they want. First of all, what is your goal, that is, how much will you be satisfied with? Second, based on the research you have done, what is the most you think the position will pay? This will be your maximum position. What is the least you will accept, or your bottom line? Once you establish your bottom line, be prepared to walk if you can't get it (see Number 12).

3. What is important to you besides money?

Are you willing to accept more nonmonetary rewards, for example, vacation time, flexible hours, permission to work from home, bigger title, more responsibility, stock options, pension plans, a bigger office, or other perks? Don't forget to consider these items as part of the overall salary picture.

4. Make time to discuss the issue.

Don't bring up the topic of your salary as an afterthought at the end of a meeting. ("Oh, by the way, there's something else I'd like to discuss with you.") Give this subject the attention it deserves. Arrange a special meeting that will focus on your salary. Get the boss to commit to a block of time.

5. Be assertive.

Don't be afraid to ask for what you want. "I think I'm worth more than you are offering/than I am being paid." If they don't agree, maybe you don't belong there. The result is always positive. Either you'll get paid what you think you're worth, or you'll discover that this isn't the right organization for you and maybe you ought to look for a better job.

6. Get the employer to make the first offer.

Like in any other negotiation, it is best to let the other person open first. If you're interviewing for the job, ask, "How much does this position pay?" If you're negotiating for a raise, ask, "How much of a raise can you approve?" She may surprise you by offering more than you expect. If she offers less, or she insists that you name a figure, ask for more than you want (see Number 7).

7. Open high.

Ask for the most you think you can reasonably expect to get—your extreme position. You can always settle for less. If you open the negotiation with your goal—what you'll merely be satisfied with—the employer may interpret this as your opening move and offer you less. When you ask for the maximum, you may get it, or at least eventually settle closer to your goal. If they say, "The salary range for this position is X to Y," you should either ask for the highest end of the range or challenge the range by explaining how you are an exception and why you deserve more.

8. Approach it from the employer's perspective.

What is your value to the employer? Don't say, "I have nine kids and a big mortgage, so I need a raise." You are not being compensated based upon your need. Frame it from the employer's point of view. Tell her what you can bring to her company and how you can impact her bottom line.

9. Get the employer to affirm your worth.

If asking your existing employer for a raise, ask your boss what he thinks of your performance. Once your boss affirms your value to the organization, he will be less resistant to giving you a raise.

10. Ask open-ended questions.

As in any negotiation, be sure to ask good questions. Be the interviewer, not the interviewee. Ask open-ended questions that require lengthy answers. "How do you feel about my performance?" "What is the company's policy on raises?" Ask your question and then shut up.

11. Let the employer do most of the talking.

Follow the 70/30 Rule: Listen 70 percent of the time and speak only 30 percent of the time. The less you talk, the more information you'll get, and the better the other person will feel about you. Remember that we all like and trust people who listen to us. Let the employer talk herself into giving you what you want.

12. Be prepared to walk.

In a salary negotiation, your willingness to walk away gives you tremendous power. If you are desperate for the job and perceive that you have no alternatives, the employer will sense your desperation. But if you're prepared to walk away if you don't get what you want, your employer will realize your worth and do whatever it takes not to lose you. And if he doesn't, the worst that can happen is you'll find another job—a BETTER job—where you will be compensated what you are worth. If you know what you want and stick to it, you will win no matter what happens.

2. LOAN RATES, MORTGAGES, AND APPROVALS

In applying for loans and mortgages, my bank has turned me down more than once. Each time I have been able to convince the bank to change its decision by providing new information or by demonstrating how its decision was based upon mistaken criteria.

My masseuse, Melissa, applied for a credit card at the bank where she had been doing business for years. They turned her down with a form letter. She called her bank manager who responded with, "Sorry, you don't have any credit history. You've never borrowed money."

"But," Melissa protested, "I have two thousand dollars in my account." He apologized again and said he could not give her a credit card. Melissa accepted the bank's decision and, six months later, decided to apply again. She got the same reply. Six months later she tried again, and again got the same negative result. Each time she accepted the rejection, she gave her negotiating power away.

Why did Melissa behave this way? Because she made several incorrect assumptions. First she assumed that, being one customer of many, she had little leverage to influence this behemoth of a corporation, that her mere two thousand dollars didn't mean much. Second, she assumed that the person she was dealing with at the bank had the last word on the subject, and so did not challenge his authority by asking to speak to a superior. Third, she assumed she had no options. If this bank turned her down, she thought, so would others.

Eventually Melissa got tired of being turned down. "Fine, don't give me a credit card," she told the bank manager. "I'll take my money, which now amounts to six thousand dollars, and go somewhere else." The manager put her on hold, and returned several minutes later with the news that she had been approved. In the end, all it took was deciding that she was willing to walk away, and it worked.

Bank officers typically have some discretion when it comes to doling out money. If you are turned down for credit, be assertive and challenge the decision. Present your point of view in a positive yet polite way. Remember that every rule has its exceptions. Resolve to be one of them. Also keep in mind that the bank wants to lend you money; after all, it doesn't make a profit on the money you don't borrow.

3. INCOME TAX

The Internal Revenue Service is more flexible than you'd think when it comes to what you should have to pay and how long you should have to pay it.

A friend of mine was audited by the IRS for a tax shelter that it ultimately decided to disallow. My friend's accountant had foreseen the difficulty and extracted my friend from the shelter before he accrued any tax liability. In spite of this, the IRS targeted him and demanded a substantial payment.

"But this issue was resolved in last year's return," my friend told the IRS examiner.

"We don't care," the examiner said. "You still owe us money."

My friend found an attorney who was able to prove that my friend had no liability, and the case was thrown out. Don't just assume you owe what the IRS says you owe. Check up on its claim, and challenge it if you think it's wrong. Failing to do so is just giving your hard-earned cash away to the government.

An important fact to bear in mind is that the tax code is not always clear. The Internal Revenue Code is a long, Byzantine document with many exemptions, loopholes, and gray areas. The vagueness of the tax code can become your weapon in negotiating with the IRS. Get yourself a good tax accountant or lawyer who understands how to maneuver within the system (legally, of course). Don't assume that the amount you owe is set in stone.

4. PROFESSIONAL FEES

Fees charged for professional services (such as your doctor, dentist, attorney, accountant, etc.) may be negotiable as well. In the medical field, fees are inflated because of our insurance system. The sob story works in this situation: "I don't have insurance and I just lost my job." Throw yourself on their mercy. Doctors and dentists are aware that many people cannot afford to pay their regular rates, and they may offer a discount. If you are not satisfied with their discount, ask:"Will you accept what the insurance company would have reimbursed you?"

Last year I was presented with a whopping lab bill of $1,800 in connection with a minor outpatient procedure. When I called to object, pointing out that my insurance would not cover it, the woman who took my call offered a suggestion: "Suppose we charge you what we would be reimbursed by the government if this were a Medicare case?" The amount: $500. By speaking up, I saved $1,300, and the lab lost nothing. A good example of win-win negotiation!

A friend of mine recently received a bill of $45,000 from her attorney for work on a divorce proceeding. But the attorney had not done a very good job, and my friend thought the amount was excessive. She turned it over to her accountant, who negotiated a deal with the lawyer by carefully itemizing each service and the extent to which it was successfully performed. The lawyer agreed to reduce the bill from $45,000 to $10,000.

Professionals typically lose a substantial percentage of their income to patients or clients who refuse or neglect to pay. If the account is turned over to a collection agency, the professional still winds up with only a small percentage of the fee, or with nothing at all. Many professionals have admitted to me that they would rather settle for something from the patient/client than have to go to a collection agency and wind up with nothing.

5. CREDIT CARD FEES

In many cases, charges such as the annual fee and even the interest rate are negotiable. Credit card companies don't advertise this sort of thing, and don't expect them to welcome your suggestions with open arms. But if you are persistent, you can negotiate a special relationship. If your company won't lower or waive the annual fee, or amend its rate policies, simply cancel the card. A friend of mine prides himself on his ability to play one card company against another. "Gizmo Card is offering me a lower interest rate," he tells them. "Will you match it?" He says they usually do. If they won't, he cancels the card and signs up with the competitor. Penalties for late payments can be negotiable as well. Try calling up with a sob story ("I misplaced the statement," or "My check must have been held up in the mail"), and they may waive the penalty.

6. CONSUMER GOODS: BUYER'S POWER

Most people don't realize the extent of their negotiating power when it comes to purchasing retail items. The typical American consumer is reluctant to challenge that retail icon, the *list price*. When I urge participants in my seminars to bargain for retail goods and services, you'd think I was asking them to commit a felony. "You can't negotiate set prices." "People will think I'm cheap." "That's not ethical." While it is considered acceptable to haggle with car dealers, for some reason the prevailing wisdom is that the same approach will not work in a department store or at the local mall. Recently a certain car manufacturer advertised that it has only one price so you won't have to be bothered with the unpleasant task of negotiating. Isn't that thoughtful of them? (Hint: NO IT ISN'T!)

Well, guess what, these rigid attitudes about wheeling and dealing are loosening up. The notion that you can stretch your paycheck by negotiating better purchases is finally enjoying wider acceptance. To prove my point, one television network turned me loose in a shopping mall. As a reporter followed me around with a hidden camera, I piled up a whopping $3,500 in discounts in just a couple of hours. The discounted items: furniture, clothing, appliances, jewelry, cell phones . . . even ice cream!

The following tips sum up my approach to getting the best deal for your money:

1. Before you negotiate, do your homework.

The same way you would read up on the dealer's cost for the car you want to buy, comparison shop to see what different stores are asking for the same type of item. Check the Internet for special Web-only deals. Investigate which products are hot and which are not; the best deals can be made on those that are less in demand.

2. Lower the seller's expectations by asking for concessions.

The only way to get a better deal is to ask for one. The more assertive you are in pursuing a better deal, the more the seller will be inclined to cave in and offer concessions. Remember that the seller is under pressure to make the sale. In many stores the salespeople are actually instructed to give a discount if the customer merely asks for one.

3. Try the Flinch.

"What! You want how much for that refrigerator? Are you crazy?" Flinching is a good way to find out if the seller's expectations are low. It may turn out that the salesperson shares your view that the price is excessive. When you flinch, he may respond with a discount.

4. Tell a Sob Story.

"I like your sofa, but I don't have enough money in my budget. I didn't plan to spend so much." This is not a lie. You have a right to set your own budget. It is the seller's choice either to accommodate it or to test your resolve by holding firm on price. The sob story is your way of testing how much he wants to make a sale.

5. Execute the Squeeze.

"I like your sofa, but I can get a better deal on it elsewhere. Will you match it?" This is also called the power of competition. Many sellers will do somersaults in order to match or beat competitive offers. Simply mentioning the competition will often lower the seller's expectations.

6. Nibble a little.

"If I buy this dress, will you throw in a pair of earrings?" The seller may not be able to discount the dress, but he can sweeten the deal by throwing in other, smaller items for free or at a reduced cost. If you are buying a sound system, ask the seller to throw in the cables. When negotiating for cell phone service, ask for the phone, carrying case, and extra minutes.

7. Buy in bulk.

"What discount will you give me if I buy two TVs instead of just one?" Most sellers are accustomed to giving bulk discounts. If you can, get a friend to buy a TV at the same time, or buy a TV and a sound system.

8. Don't limit your bargaining to price.

You can also negotiate for items such as better terms (a discount for paying cash; postponed billing), free delivery and installation, and a free or extended warranty.

9. Be patient and persistent.

If the seller says no, don't give up. Sometimes the best deal will come only after you have devoted some time to the negotiation. Persistence convinces the seller that you are serious. A friend of mine spends four hours or more at the dealer each time he buys a new car. He wears the salesperson down.

10. Walk out.

Your willingness to walk out and spend your money elsewhere is your greatest asset in any bargaining situation. Many great deals occur when you return the second or third time. A salesperson may even run after you as you attempt to leave. Give him your business card so he can call you with a better deal.

11. Wait for the seller's big sale or slow season.

Timing is everything. Many clothing, appliance, and furniture stores substantially slash prices at least once a year, usually after January 1. When buying a car, consider visiting the dealer on a rainy day at the end of the month when dealer traffic is light. Or buy at the end of the model year, after next year's models have been introduced. I just bought a set of audio speakers at one-third of the regular price because the model had just been discontinued. The difference is cosmetic—the speakers have a new logo on the front. They are still great speakers. If a sale has just ended, ask for the sale price anyway. Or if a sale is coming in the near future, ask if you buy the item now at full price, will the dealer agree to refund the difference between your price and the sale price once the sale begins.

12. Ask for advice.

If you politely ask the salesperson for suggestions on how you can get a better deal, she may surprise you with ideas you never thought of. She is in a position to know how the store has given concessions in the past, or the dates of an upcoming sale. Even if she doesn't have the authority to deal, her ideas can help you bargain with the manager.

13. Go to a higher level.

If the salesperson can't or won't give you the deal you want, ask to see the manager or owner. Higher-ups are more likely to bargain because they have more authority, they have less time to haggle, and they are more inclined to look at big-picture issues such as customer goodwill and inventory requirements. Also, the amount of your requested discount may seem less significant to a manager, who is used to looking at overall sales figures, than to the salesperson, who is focused on her commission.

14. Find a way for the seller to save face.

Some sellers may be reluctant to give you a discount because they feel they will have to do so for the next customer. You can give them a way out by accepting a product with a defect, or by choosing the floor model, last year's model, or a repossession. Help them justify making an exception.

15. Be charming and funny.

Salespeople will go out of their way to help a friendly customer. The use of humor can lighten up the atmosphere, weaken the seller's defenses, and make it easier for you to assume a tough bargaining position without alienating the salesperson.

Remember: None of these techniques will work unless you convince yourself that it is okay to negotiate. When you bargain for goods and services, you are participating in one of the oldest human activities. The people who founded this country were traders who wheeled and dealed all the time. In most other parts of the world, bargaining is a respected art form that is enjoyed by both buyer and seller in many different settings.

7. HOTEL RATES

Hotels typically offer corporate rates, senior rates, AAA rates, and weekend rates that are far better than the rate offered to the traveler off the street (the "rack" rate). Ask for these. Remember, hotels do not like to have empty rooms. Even if none of these rates apply to you, tell them what you'd like to spend—they may offer you a special rate that you didn't even know existed. I tried this recently in Munich, Germany. Even though I had arrived at a busy time (Oktoberfest) without a reservation, I was able to get a room at half the advertised price merely by saying, "I'd love to stay here, but all I can afford to spend is blah-blah-blah." The hotel clerk agreed. My friend booked a four-star hotel in New York (where hotel rooms are notoriously expensive) by bidding online. In the end, he stayed in a $500-per-night room for only $135.

You can use the power of competition: "I like your hotel, but I can get a better room rate elsewhere." Or you can try a nibble: "If you won't lower the room rate, will you waive the parking fee? Or give us an upgraded room?"

8. VACATION PACKAGES

Vacation packages advertised by travel agencies are always subject to change. Often these rates hinge on world events. After a month of rioting in France, or terrorist attacks in Bali, or a tsunami on Phuket, don't you think the travel companies were willing to offer discounted packages to those locations? You should consider their advertised rates merely a guess about what the market will bear. By negotiating, you will discover their bottom line.

9. AIRLINE TICKETS AND SERVICES

These days, dozens of sites offer bargain fares! Comparison shop among several of these sites and try searching for fares on a variety of dates. Most travelers don't know that flights are often cheaper if you include a Saturday night stay, book two weeks in advance, or wait for last-minute bargain fares. Once you've gotten a good deal on your flight, there's nothing to keep you from negotiating for an upgrade.

Recently I was notified by mail that I had failed to qualify for this year's elite status in one of the airline frequent flyer programs to which I belong because I had not accrued the necessary number of airline miles the previous year. In this situation most people would say, "Okay, that's too bad, but that's the way it is." Not me. So I called the airline and requested to be bumped into elite. The first person I talked to told me politely that unless I had the qualifying number of miles, *she did not have the authority* to do what I asked. I thanked her, hung up, and called again. The second person I spoke with said, "Sorry, *it is against the policy of the airline* to award elite status if you don't have the required number of miles in your account." I hung up and called again. The third person who answered said, "Why Mr. Brodow, I see that you have had elite status for many years. Of course we can go ahead and give you elite status for this year. *No problem!*" This happened only because I challenged the airline's position and didn't back down.

10. DIVORCE SETTLEMENTS

In the case of a divorce settlement, emotional trauma often prevents participants from treating the negotiation like any other business transaction, which it is. Negotiation strategies—such as making extreme offers, lowering the other side's aspirations, setting high goals, and being willing to walk away—work just as well in a divorce settlement as in any other negotiation. The big danger in divorce proceedings is the hefty bill your attorney is preparing for you. Try to limit the extent to which the lawyers get involved. If the two of you can work it out yourselves without the lawyers, you will have more assets to divide. And be proactive when negotiating the fee with your lawyer. It is not cast in stone.

IT WORKS!

I am pleased to recount what happened to the woman who fought with me about negotiating for retail items. When our seminar broke for lunch, she walked across the street to a shopping mall and bought an expensive pair of sunglasses. She returned to the seminar and reported that she had convinced the store salesperson to reduce the price of the glasses from $175 to $115.

Although it won't work every time, bargaining is successful often enough to make it worthwhile and a whole lot of fun. The bottom line is that if you don't negotiate, you are unnecessarily leaving much of your hard-earned money on the table. If you don't ask, you don't get.

BONUS CATEGORY: NEGOTIATING IN PERSONAL RELATIONSHIPS

As Boot Camp draws to a close, don't forget that we negotiate not only in business, but also with friends and family. We negotiate constantly over where we meet for dinner, what to shop for, where to vacation, and more. And often these negotiations can be more important than those we conduct in business because they involve a commodity that is even more valuable than money—your time. One reason we have so many catastrophes in our personal lives is that we fail to apply the same rules of cooperative negotiating— like remembering to listen actively, being patient and flexible, and focusing on reaching an agreement that will satisfy *both* sides—to negotiating with our loved ones. We seem to think that the people in our lives—mother, father, wife, husband, sister, son, best friend—will be there no matter what, so it really doesn't matter how we treat them. Not so. If you want peace and amity in your private life, simply follow the Three Rules for Win-Win Negotiating:

1. *Change your behavior from adversarial to cooperative*. Treat your loved ones with respect. Don't assume the worst about their motives—try to understand their wacky behavior. Stop yelling at them if you disagree.
2. *Develop trust by listening*. If you follow the 70/30 Rule and let your spouse—or child or parent or friend—do most of the talking, they will be reminded that you care about them and will be more cooperative in how they interact with you.
3. *Explore options for mutual satisfaction*. Instead of barking orders, let your loved ones have a say in making decisions. Brainstorm possible solutions to your disagreements. Compromise. If you can't reach agreement, bring in an expert, such as a therapist, attorney, or financial adviser.

The ideas in this book have the potential to make you a very powerful person. By being a good negotiator, you can exercise amazing control in all aspects of your life and, if you follow the rules for cooperative negotiation, find a more amiable, enjoyable way of getting what you want, both in business and in your personal life.

Customizing Your Own Negotiation Strategy

DETERMINING YOUR NEGOTIATION QUOTIENT

Rate yourself on each of the Ten Traits of Successful Negotiators:

		Excellent				Needs Work
1.	Negotiation Consciousness	5	4	3	2	1
2.	Listening Well	5	4	3	2	1
3.	Having High Aspirations	5	4	3	2	1
4.	Being a Detective: Asking Questions	5	4	3	2	1
5.	Exercising Patience	5	4	3	2	1
6.	Flexible Assumptions	5	4	3	2	1
7.	Focusing on Satisfaction	5	4	3	2	1
8.	Taking Risks	5	4	3	2	1
9.	Problem-Solving	5	4	3	2	1
10.	Willingness to Walk Away	5	4	3	2	1

If you manage to score well in all categories—a 40 or above cumulative score—congratulations. If you fall below that, or are weak in a few areas, use this test as a way to zero in on the areas in which you need improvement.

MAPPING OUT YOUR NEXT NEGOTIATION

1. What are your targets?

- **Determine Your Maximum Position:** The best outcome you think you could possibly attain in the negotiation.
- **Set Your Goal:** The result you'd be satisfied to achieve in this negotiation.
- **Determine Your Minimum Position (Bottom Line):** The worst outcome you will accept in order to make a deal. Anything short of this and you will walk away.

2. What are your needs, that is, what do you need to achieve?

3. What are your options? Do you have a Plan B?

4. What concessions are you willing to make?

5. What pressure is there on the other side to make a deal?

6. How can you help the other side feel satisfied—without giving away too much?

7. What is your opening position?

8. Where should the negotiation be held?

9. How many people should be present?

10. What interests do both sides have in common?

11. What options exist for mutual satisfaction?

ED BRODOW is the nation's most innovative expert on the art of negotiation. Millions of television viewers and more than a thousand audiences in North and South America, Europe, and Asia have benefited from his practical ideas on making deals. He is the creator of Negotiation Boot Camp™, widely recognized as the number one customized negotiating skills seminar in the United States. Ed's other books include *Negotiate with Confidence* and *Beating the Success Trap: Negotiating for the Life You Really Want and the Rewards You Deserve*.

As a nationally recognized television personality, Ed has appeared as negotiation guru on Fox News, *Inside Edition*, PBS, *Fortune Business Report* (New York), and KRON-TV4 (San Francisco). His two-hour PBS special, "Negotiate with Confidence," garnered rave reviews. His ideas on negotiating have been showcased in the *Washington Post, LA Times, Wall Street Journal, Entrepreneur, Men's Health, Cosmo-*

politan, Professional Speaker, SmartMoney, Reader's Digest, and *Selling Power*.

For more than a decade, Ed's Negotiation Boot Camp seminars have sharpened the deal-making skills of thousands of executives from senior management, sales, purchasing, legal, customer service, contracts, marketing, engineering, insurance, and other business world competencies. His impressive client list includes American Express, Baker Hughes, Cessna Aircraft, Cisco Systems, ConAgra, DaimlerChrysler, The Gap, Goldman Sachs, The Hartford, Hyatt Hotels, IBM, Johnson & Johnson, Kimberly-Clark, KPMG Peat Marwick, Learjet, McDonald's, Microsoft, Mobil Oil, National Contract Management Association, the Pentagon, Philip Morris, Quest Diagnostics, Raytheon, Revlon, Seagate, Starbucks, Sun Microsystems, Symantec, 3M, TRW, Turnaround Management Association, and Zurich Insurance.

In previous careers Ed was a corporate sales executive (IBM, Litton Industries), Marine Corps officer, and movie actor with roles opposite Jessica Lange, Ron Howard, and Christopher Reeve. He is a member of Screen Actors Guild and National Speakers Association. A graduate of Brooklyn College (City University of New York), Ed lives by the sea in Monterey, California.

To book Ed Brodow as the speaker at
your meeting or convention:

ed@brodow.com
www.brodow.com